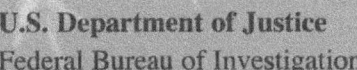

U.S. Department of Justice
Federal Bureau of Investigation

TERRORISM
2002–2005

TERR⊕RISM
2002-2005

FOREWORD

TERRORISM 2002-2005

Since the mid-1980s, the FBI has published *Terrorism in the United States*, an unclassified annual report summarizing terrorist activities in this country. While this publication provided an overview of the terrorist threat in the United States and its territories, its limited scope proved inadequate for conveying either the breadth or width of the terrorist threat facing U.S. interests or the scale of the FBI's response to terrorism worldwide. To better reflect the nature of the threat and the international scope of our response, the FBI expanded the focus of its annual terrorism report in the 2000/2001 edition to include discussion of FBI investigations overseas and renamed the series *Terrorism*.

This second edition of *Terrorism* provides an overview of the terrorist incidents and preventions designated by the FBI as having taken place in the United States and its territories during the years 2002 through 2005 and that are matters of public record. This publication does not include those incidents which the Bureau classifies under criminal rather than terrorism investigations. In addition, the report discusses major FBI investigations overseas and identifies significant events—including legislative actions, prosecutorial updates, and program developments—relevant to U.S. counterterrorism efforts. The report concludes with an "In Focus" article summarizing the history of the FBI's counterterrorism program.

While the discussion of international terrorism provides a more complete overview of FBI terrorism investigations into acts involving U.S. interests around the world, *Terrorism* is not intended as a comprehensive annual review of worldwide terrorist activity. The chronological incidents, charts, and figures included in *Terrorism 2002-2005* reflect only those incidents identified in the *Terrorism/Terrorism in the United States* series. For more complete listings of worldwide terrorist incidents, see the Worldwide Incidents Tracking System maintained by the National Counterterrorism Center at *www.nctc.gov* and the Terrorism Knowledge Base compiled by the Memorial Institute for the Prevention of Terrorism at *www.tkb.org*.

The FBI hopes you will find *Terrorism 2002-2005* to be a helpful resource and thanks you for your interest in the FBI's Counterterrorism Program. A full-text and graphics version of this issue, as well as recent back issues of *Terrorism* and *Terrorism in the United States*, are available for on-line reference on the FBI home page at *www.fbi.gov*.

Federal Bureau of Investigation
Counterterrorism Division

n accordance with U.S. counterterrorism policy, the FBI considers terrorists to be criminals. FBI efforts in countering terrorist threats are multifaceted. Information obtained through FBI investigations is analyzed and used to prevent terrorist activity and, whenever possible, to effect the arrest and prosecution of potential perpetrators. FBI investigations are initiated in accordance with the following guidelines:

FBI POLICY AND GUIDELINES

- Domestic terrorism investigations are conducted in accordance with *The Attorney General's Guidelines on General Crimes, Racketeering Enterprise, and Terrorism Enterprise Investigations*. These guidelines set forth the predication threshold and limits for investigations of U.S. persons who reside in the United States, who are not acting on behalf of a foreign power, and who may be conducting criminal activities in support of terrorist objectives.

- International terrorism investigations are conducted in accordance with *The Attorney General Guidelines for FBI Foreign Intelligence Collection and Foreign Counterintelligence Investigations*. These guidelines set forth the predication level and limits for investigating U.S. persons or foreign nationals in the United States who are targeting national security interests on behalf of a foreign power.

Although various Executive Orders, Presidential Decision Directives, and congressional statutes address the issue of terrorism, there is no single federal law specifically making terrorism a crime. Terrorists are arrested and convicted under existing criminal statutes. All suspected terrorists placed under arrest are provided access to legal counsel and normal judicial procedure, including Fifth Amendment guarantees.

DEFINITIONS

There is no single, universally accepted, definition of terrorism. Terrorism is defined in the *Code of Federal Regulations* as "the unlawful use of force and violence against persons or property to intimidate or coerce a government, the civilian population, or any segment thereof, in furtherance of political or social objectives" (28 C.F.R. Section 0.85).

The FBI further describes terrorism as either domestic or international, depending on the origin, base, and objectives of the terrorist organization. For the purpose of this report, the FBI will use the following definitions:

- Domestic terrorism is the unlawful use, or threatened use, of force or violence by a group or individual based and operating entirely within the United States or Puerto Rico without foreign direction committed against persons or property to intimidate or coerce a government, the civilian population, or any segment thereof in furtherance of political or social objectives.

- International terrorism involves violent acts or acts dangerous to human life that are a violation of the criminal laws of the United States or any state, or that would be a criminal violation if committed within the jurisdiction of the United States or any state. These acts appear to be intended to intimidate or coerce a civilian population, influence the policy of a government by intimidation or coercion, or affect the conduct of a government by assassination or kidnapping. International terrorist acts occur outside the United States or transcend national boundaries in terms of the means by which they are accomplished, the persons they appear intended to coerce or intimidate, or the locale in which their perpetrators operate or seek asylum.

THE FBI DIVIDES TERRORIST-RELATED ACTIVITY INTO TWO CATEGORIES:

- A terrorist *incident* is a violent act or an act dangerous to human life, in violation of the criminal laws of the United States, or of any state, to intimidate or coerce a government, the civilian population, or any segment thereof, in furtherance of political or social objectives.

- A terrorism *prevention* is a documented instance in which a violent act by a known or suspected terrorist group or individual with the means and a proven propensity for violence is successfully interdicted through investigative activity.

NOTE

The FBI investigates terrorism-related matters without regard to race, religion, national origin, or gender. Reference to individual members of any political, ethnic, or religious group in this report is not meant to imply that all members of that group are terrorists. Terrorists represent a small criminal minority in any larger social context.

TABLE of CONTENTS

INTRODUCTION

This edition of *Terrorism* highlights significant terrorism-related events in the United States and selected FBI investigative efforts overseas that occurred during the years 2002 through 2005. Additionally, this report provides a wide range of statistical data relating to terrorism in the United States during the past two decades. This material is presented to provide readers with an historical framework for the examination of contemporary terrorism issues.

TERRORISM 2002-2005

In keeping with a longstanding trend, domestic extremists carried out the majority of terrorist incidents during this period. Twenty three of the 24 recorded terrorist incidents were perpetrated by domestic terrorists. With the exception of a white supremacist's firebombing of a synagogue in Oklahoma City, Oklahoma, all of the domestic terrorist incidents were committed by special interest extremists active in the animal rights and environmental movements. The acts committed by these extremists typically targeted materials and facilities rather than persons. The sole international terrorist incident in the United States recorded for this period involved an attack at the El Al ticket counter at Los Angeles International Airport, which claimed the lives of two victims.

The terrorism preventions for 2002 through 2005 present a more diverse threat picture. Eight of the 14 recorded terrorism preventions stemmed from right-wing extremism, and included disruptions to plotting by individuals involved with the militia, white supremacist, constitutionalist and tax protestor, and anti-abortion movements. The remaining preventions included disruptions to plotting by an anarchist in Bellingham, Washington, who sought to bomb a U.S. Coast Guard station; a plot to attack an Islamic center in Pinellis Park, Florida; and a plot by prison-originated, Muslim convert group to attack U.S. military, Jewish, and Israeli targets in the greater Los Angeles area. In addition, three preventions involved individuals who sought to provide material support to foreign terrorist organizations, including al-Qa'ida, for attacks within the United States.

Whereas the violent global jihadist movement manifested itself primarily in terrorism preventions in the United States from 2002 through 2005, internationally the movement claimed major attacks against U.S. and Western targets that resulted in American casualties. Most of these incidents were perpetrated by regional jihadist groups operating in primarily Muslim countries, and included attacks committed by Indonesia-based Jemaah Islamiya and al-Qa'ida in the Arabian Peninsula. The coordinated suicide bombing of London's mass transit system by homegrown jihadists, however, brought the violent jihadist movement and the tactic of suicide bombing to a major European capital.

In addition to these incidents and preventions, the years 2002 through 2005 saw the resolutions to high-profile prosecutions in the fight against terrorism. These included the October 4, 2002, sentencing of John Walker Lindh to 20 years in prison for conspiring with the Taliban to kill U.S. citizens; the January 30, 2003, sentencing of Richard Colvin Reid to life in prison for attempting to bomb a transcontinental flight using a shoe bomb; the December 2003 sentencings of the Lackawanna Six terror cell members, who received prison terms ranging from seven to 10 years for providing material support or resources to al-Qa'ida; the sentencings in 2003 and 2004 of members of a Portland terrorist cell, who received prison terms ranging from three to 18 years for plotting to provide assistance to the Taliban and al-Qa'ida in fighting against U.S. troops in Afghanistan; the September 29, 2004, sentencing in Yemeni court of six individuals for their roles in the *USS Cole* bombing, two of whom received the death penalty; the April 6, 2005, sentencing of Matthew Hale, leader of the white supremacist Creativity Movement, to 40 years in prison for solicitation of violence and obstruction of justice; the July 18, 2005, sentencing of Eric Robert Rudolph to life in prison for perpetrating several bombings, including the Centennial Olympic Park bombing in Atlanta, Georgia; the April 26, 2005, sentencing of Ali Al-Timimi to life in prison for encouraging others to receive military training from the designated foreign terrorist organization Lashkar-e-Tayyiba to fight U.S. troops in Afghanistan; and the August 30, 2005, sentencing of white supremacist Sean Michael Gillespie to 39 years for the synagogue firebombing in Oklahoma City.

FBI counterterrorism initiatives since the 9/11 terrorist attack have focused on preventing future attacks through the timely gathering, analysis, and dissemination of information; the facilitation of appropriate sharing of terrorism-related information between federal, state, and local partners; and the advancement of intelligence and law enforcement partnerships worldwide. FBI and U.S. counterterrorism organizational changes from 2002 through 2005 include the creation of the National Joint Terrorism Task Force; the establishment of the Foreign Terrorist Tracking Task Force; the consolidation of government terrorist watch lists into the Terrorist Screening Center; the creation of the U.S. Department of Homeland Security; and the restructuring of the U.S. Intelligence Community under the newly created Office of the Director of National Intelligence. These and other federal initiatives are discussed in greater detail in the concluding In Focus retrospective of the FBI's counterterrorism program.

The FBI recorded seven domestic terrorist incidents, one international terrorist incident, and one terrorism prevention in 2002. The seven domestic terrorism incidents included a string of attacks over a period of several months claimed by special interest movements. These attacks are attributed either solely to the Earth Liberation Front (ELF), an extremist environmental movement active in the United States during the past 20 years, or jointly to the ELF and the Animal Liberation Front, an extremist animal rights movement that has carried out numerous terrorist attacks since 1987. The international terrorist incident involved fatal shootings at the El Al ticket counter at Los Angeles International Airport.

In the one terrorism prevention, law enforcement in Florida exposed a plot to attack Islamic facilities in the United States in response to international events, including the September 11 attacks.

Two deaths resulted from terrorist activity carried out in the United States in 2002.

A major international terrorist incident during 2002 involved the October 12 bombing of the Kuta Beach nightclub area on Bali, Indonesia. The attack, carried out by the Jemaah Islamiya, a terrorist organization active in Southeast Asia, resulted in 202 deaths, including those of seven Americans.

2002 TERRORIST INCIDENTS

MARCH 2002 – NOVEMBER 2002
Vandalism and Arson
Erie, Harborcreek, and Warren, Pennsylvania
(*Six acts of Domestic Terrorism*)

Between March 2002 and November 2002, a series of animal rights and ecoterrorism incidents occurred in Erie, Harborcreek, and Warren, Pennsylvania. On March 18, 2002, Pennsylvania State Police discovered heavy equipment used to clear trees at a construction site in Erie, Pennsylvania, spray painted with the statements "ELF, in the protection of mother earth," and "Stop Deforestation." On March 24, 2002, police responded to the same construction site, where a large hydraulic crane had been set on fire, causing approximately $500,000 in damage. A facsimile, purportedly from ELF, claimed responsibility for the arson and vandalism. ELF also claimed responsibility for an August 11, 2002, arson on the U.S. Forestry Scientific Laboratory in Warren, Pennsylvania.

In separate incidents in May and September 2002, unknown subjects released approximately 250 mink from a fur farm in Harborcreek, Pennsylvania. On November 26, 2002, the barn on the same Harborcreek fur farm was destroyed by arson. On the ELF Web site, ELF and ALF jointly claimed responsibility for these mink releases and the arson. On August 11, 2002, unknown individuals committed arson on the U.S. Forestry Scientific Laboratory in Warren, Pennsylvania.

JULY 4, 2002
Attack on El Al Ticket Counter in Los Angeles International Airport
Los Angeles, California
(One act of International Terrorism)

On July 4, 2002, Hesham Mohamed Ali Hedayat began shooting randomly while standing in line at the ticket counter of El Al Israeli National Airlines at the Los Angeles International Airport. During the attack, an El Al ticketing agent and a bystander were killed. Hedayat was subsequently killed by an El Al security officer. A worldwide investigation determined that Hadayat's religious and political beliefs were the primary motivation for the attack, and not personal revenge. Following these investigative findings, this case was officially designated as an act of international terrorism.

AUGUST – OCTOBER 2002
Vandalism and Destruction of Property
Henrico County, Virginia
Goochland County, Virginia
(One act of Domestic Terrorism)

During the period of August–November 2002, Aaron L. Linas, John B. Wade, and Adam V. Blackwell carried out several acts of vandalism and destruction of private property, in apparent acts of environmental terrorism. Many of these acts were attributed to the Earth Liberation Front (ELF).

On several days in August 2002, the individuals damaged 12 construction vehicles at a construction site in Goochland, Virginia, by pouring sugar into the gas tanks. The individuals also vandalized two homes under construction in the area, writing the word "sprawl" on one of the homes.

In September 2002, the individuals vandalized construction vehicles in Henrico County, Virginia, and attempted to burn a backhoe and construction crane. On September 28, 2002, 25 sport utility vehicles (SUVs) were damaged at an Henrico County Ford Dealership, including the etching of the letters "ELF" and "SUV" into some of the vehicles. Also in September, vandalism occurred at two fast food restaurants. A Jeep Liberty was also damaged, and the vandals left a note on the vehicle stating "SUVs are killing the world" and "Earth Liberation Front."

In October of 2002, vandals claiming to be part of ELF apparently used an axe to damage three SUVs parked in the River Lake Colony subdivision of Henrico County, Virginia. Notes were left on all of the vehicles claiming the attack was an effort to raise environmental and political awareness.

Linas, Wade, and Blackwell pled guilty to conspiracy to commit these acts and were subsequently convicted and sentenced to three years and six months, three years and one month, and 10 months in federal prison, respectively, and ordered to divide the total restitution payment of $204,021.86 between them.

2002 TERRORISM PREVENTIONS

AUGUST 22, 2002
Planned Attack against Islamic Center of Pinellas County
Pinellas Park, Florida
(Prevention of one act of Domestic Terrorism)

On August 22, 2002, police in Pinellas County, Florida, responding to a domestic dispute detained Robert J. Goldstein after finding numerous weapons and explosives and a "mission statement" threatening to attack Islamic facilities in the United States. Goldstein was later arrested and charged with weapons violations and an attempt to destroy property. Michael Wallace Hardee, Samuel V. Shannahan III, and Goldstein's wife, Kristi Goldstein, were also arrested and charged in connection with the plot. An investigation revealed that the intended target of Goldstein's planned attack was the Islamic Center of Pinellas County, in Pinellas Park, Florida, and that the attack had been planned to coincide with the first anniversary of the September 11, 2001, terrorist attack. Investigators also determined that Goldstein intended to target the Islamic Center in perceived retaliation for Palestinian suicide bombings in Israel. The four pled guilty in the Middle District of Florida to their roles in the plotting, and in 2003 received federal prison sentences ranging from three years to Robert Goldstein's 12 years and seven months.

2002 SIGNIFICANT EVENTS

JANUARY 19, 2002
Kathleen Ann Soliah Sentenced

On January 19, 2002, Kathleen Ann Soliah was sentenced to two consecutive 10 years to life terms for her role in a 1975 car bombing plot associated with the Symbionese Liberation Army. On October 31, 2001, Soliah pled guilty to two counts related to the car bombing plot. Soliah remained a fugitive for 23 years until her arrest on June 16, 1999, when she was living under the alias Sara Jane Olsen.

MARCH 14, 2002
Appeal Denied in the Pan Am 103 Bombing Case

On March 14, 2002, an appeal filed by Abdel Basset Ali Al-Megrahi, seeking to overturn his conviction of bombing Pan Am flight 103 over Lockerbie, Scotland, was denied. Al-Megrahi had filed the appeal at the Scottish Court of Appeal in Camp Zeist, The Netherlands. Al-Megrahi was convicted on January 31, 2001, for the 1988 bombing, which killed the 259 passengers of the flight and 11 individuals on the ground. Al-Megrahi was sentenced to life in prison.

JUNE 15, 2002
Donald Rudolph Sentenced for 1999 Propane Plot

On June 15, 2002, Donald Rudolph was sentenced to five years in prison for his role in a plot to destroy a propane storage facility near Elk Grove, California. Rudolph had pled guilty on January 19, 2001, to withholding knowledge of a conspiracy to use a weapon of mass destruction in connection with the propane plot.

The plot to attack the propane storage facility was disrupted on December 3, 1999, when members of the Sacramento Joint Terrorism Task Force arrested Kevin Ray Patterson and Charles Dennis Kiles. Patterson, Kiles, and Rudolph were associated with an antigovernment group active in the central region of the state. When arrested, Patterson and Kiles were in possession of a detonation cord, blasting caps, grenade hulls, and various chemicals—including ammonium nitrate—and

OCTOBER 12, 2002
Nightclub Bombing
Bali, Indonesia

On October 12, 2002, three bombs, including a large vehicle bomb and a possible suicide bomber, devastated a nightclub area at Kuta Beach on the Indonesian island of Bali. The blasts killed 202 people, including seven Americans, and injured as many as 350. Most of those killed and injured were foreign tourists. This bombing has been attributed to members of the Jemaah Islamiya (JI) terrorist organization, a Southeast Asian-based terrorist network with links to al-Qa'ida, which allegedly helped finance the attack. The Bali bombing may have been carried out in response to audiotaped appeals from al-Qa'ida leader Usama Bin Ladin and his senior deputy Ayman al-Zawahiri broadcast on the al-Jazeera network beginning on October 6, 2002, that urged renewed attacks on U.S. and Western interests.

The FBI joined several other international antiterror agencies to assist Indonesia in the investigation of the attack. The investigation has yielded approximately 30 convictions overseas; including three suspects sentenced to death after being convicted of planning and carrying out the bombing. Notable among the convictions is Muslim cleric Abu Bakar Bashir, who is suspected of being the spiritual leader of JI. Bashir was sentenced in March 2003 to 30 months in prison for his part in the criminal conspiracy leading to the attack, although he was cleared of charges of planning a terrorist attack.

Investigators believe JI militants Noordin Mohammad Top and bomb-maker Azahari Husin were the masterminds behind the Bali nightclub attacks and several other Southeast Asian terrorist attacks. Husin was killed by Indonesian police during a shootout on November 9, 2005, in East Java, Indonesia. Top remained a fugitive at the end of 2005.

On October 23, 2002, President George W. Bush designated JI as a Specially Designated Global Terrorist (SDGT) under Executive Order 13224. Investigation into the Bali bombing is ongoing.

numerous weapons. Patterson and Kiles were convicted in May 2002 for conspiracy to use a weapon of mass destruction and conspiracy to use a destructive device.

JUNE 21, 2002
Two Smugglers Convicted in Terror Financing Case

On June 21, 2002, Mohamad Hammoud and Chawki Hammoud were convicted for their roles in a Charlotte, North Carolina-based, cigarette smuggling ring with ties to terrorism financing. Both men were convicted of cigarette smuggling, money laundering, racketeering, and credit card fraud. Mohamad Hammoud was also convicted of providing financial support to Hizballah, a designated foreign terrorist organization believed to have received financing through Hammoud's smuggling enterprise. Chawki Hammoud was not found guilty of Hizballah ties.

JUNE 21, 2002
FBI Fly Team Established

On June 21, 2002, FBI Director Mueller announced the creation of the Fly Team in the Counterterrorism Division to enhance the Bureau's capabilities in the areas of counterterrorism and intelligence collection. The Fly Team deploys rapidly and proactively worldwide on missions to identify and prevent acts of terrorism, respond to crisis incidents, and pursue the arrests and prosecutions of terrorists who have engaged in or aided and abetted those who engaged in acts of terrorism.

JULY 2002
Creation of National Joint Terrorism Task Force

In July of 2002, the National Joint Terrorism Task Force (NJTTF) was created by order of the Director of the FBI. The NJTTF, staffed by representatives from 40 federal, state, and local agencies, is tasked with coordinating the flow of information between its participating entities and the Joint Terrorism Task Forces (JTTFs) located in FBI field offices and resident agencies across the country.

OCTOBER 4, 2002
John Walker Lindh Sentenced

On October 4, 2002, U.S. citizen John Walker Lindh was sentenced to 20 years in prison after pleading guilty in July to terrorism charges related to his association with the Taliban in Afghanistan. In February, a grand jury in the Eastern District of Virginia indicted Lindh on 10 counts, charging him as an al-Qa'ida-trained terrorist who conspired with the Taliban to kill U.S. citizens. In addition to criminal charges that had previously been levied against Lindh, the indictment added charges of conspiracy to contribute services to al-Qa'ida, contributing services to al-Qa'ida, conspiracy to supply services to the Taliban, and weapons charges.

NOVEMBER 25, 2002
Signing of the Homeland Security Act of 2002

On November 25, 2002, President Bush signed House Resolution 5005, the Homeland Security Act of 2002, officially establishing the U.S. Department of Homeland Security. The act combined various government agencies dealing with transportation, border, and other security issues from the U.S. Departments of Justice, Defense, Treasury, and Commerce into a single cabinet department, consolidating the U.S. government's homeland security efforts.

2003 IN REVIEW

n 2003, the FBI recorded six terrorist incidents and five terrorism preventions. Domestic terrorists, specifically animal rights and environmental extremists, were responsible for each of the six incidents. Three of the incidents were perpetrated by followers of the Earth Liberation Front extremist movement and involved acts of arson or vandalism and destruction of property. The other three incidents were perpetrated by extremists within the animal rights movement, and included and act of vandalism claimed by the Animal Liberation Front, and two bombings at businesses affiliated with Huntingdon Life Sciences, a frequent target of the extreme animal rights movement.

Each of the five preventions involved domestic terrorist organizations or extremists. These included a white supremacist in Pennsylvania, who planned attacks against abortion clinics and minority targets; a constitutionalist and tax protestor in Idaho, who attempted to arrange for the murders of federal persons involved in a tax evasion case against him; an individual in Texas associated with antigovernment militia members, who was found in possession of heavy weaponry, sodium cyanide, and plans to weaponize sodium cyanide; an anarchist, who planned to bomb a U.S. Coast Guard; and an anti-abortion extremist in Florida, who planned to bomb abortion clinics.

No deaths or serious injuries resulted from terrorist activity carried out in the United States in 2003.

Major international terrorist incidents involving U.S. casualties included two attacks stemming from the violent global jihadist movement. In Riyadh, Saudi Arabia, al-Qa'ida operatives conducted coordinated assaults on three residential compounds housing Western workers. Nine of the 35 people killed in the attack were Americans. In addition, Jemaah Islamiya bombed the JW Marriott Hotel in Jakarta, Indonesia. The attack resulted in 11 fatalities and 144 injuries, including injuries to two U.S. citizens.

2003 TERRORIST INCIDENTS

JANUARY 1, 2003
Arson
Girard, Pennsylvania
(One act of Domestic Terrorism)

On January 1, 2003, an unknown individual(s) set two pickup trucks and one sport utility vehicle on fire at a car dealership in Girard, Pennsylvania, causing $96,000 in damages. This arson followed the series of environmental and animal rights extremist incidents in northwest Pennsylvania discussed in the preceding 2002 terrorist incidents section. ELF claimed responsibility for the arson.

MARCH 3, 2003
Vandalism
Chico, California
(One act of Domestic Terrorism)

On March 3, 2003, an unknown number of individuals placed two one-gallon jugs filled with kerosene near a McDonald's restaurant in Chico, California, and vandalized the restaurant with graffiti. The graffiti included statements such as "Animal Liberation Front," "Meat is Murder," and "Species Equality." Two communiques were discovered claiming responsibility for the attack. Robert Brooks and Harjit Singh Gill were convicted in the Eastern District of California for making false statements to a grand jury in connection with the attack, and, in June 2005, received sentences of a $500 fine and 36 months probation, respectively.

AUGUST 1, 2003
SEPTEMBER 19, 2003
Arson
San Diego, California
(One act of Domestic Terrorism)

On August 1, 2003, the San Diego Fire Department and San Diego Police Department responded to an arson fire at the Garden Condominium, a five-story, 206-unit condominium complex under construction in the University Town Center area of San Diego. The fire caused an estimated $20 million in damages to the building and surrounding construction equipment. Investigators found graffiti at the site implicating Earth Liberation Front (ELF) extremists with the incident, including the message "IF YOU BUILD IT – WE WILL BURN IT. THE ELF'S ARE MAD.·

On September 19, 2003, two other new home sites were also set on fire, with similar messages left at the scene. The fires destroyed four homes and damaged two others, causing an estimated loss of $3 million. The August 1 and September 19 arson incidents remain under investigation.

MAY 12, 2003
Bombings of Residential Compounds
Riyadh, Saudi Arabia

On the evening of May 12, 2003, al-Qa'ida operatives assaulted three residential compounds in Riyadh, Saudi Arabia, that house Western guest workers. At least fifteen assailants in six vehicles-two vehicles at each location-participated in the attacks against the Al-Hamra Oasis Village, Jedawal compound, and Vinnell Company compound located in suburban Riyadh. After breaching manned security barriers at two of the three sites, the attackers detonated vehicle-borne improvised explosive devices (VBIEDs) in the compounds, killing 35 people, including nine Americans, and injuring nearly 200 others. This assault followed a string of al-Qa'ida operations, including the August 7, 1998, East African embassy bombings; the October 12, 2000, bombing of the USS Cole in Aden, Yemen; the September 11, 2001, attack in the United States; and attacks on November 28, 2002, carried out against primarily Israeli targets in Mombasa, Kenya, involving simultaneous attacks against multiple targets.

The May 12 attack reflected a high degree of planning, pre-operational surveillance, and coordination among teams—traditional hallmarks of al-Qa'ida operations. It also reflected a highly refined approach to suicide bombings that may have incorporated lessons learned from the 1998 U.S. embassy bombings and other attacks. Preliminary investigation indicates that operatives traveling in lead vehicles attacked guards at each of the sites with small arms fire and hand grenades to quickly breach gates and other security measures to gain access to the compounds. Once inside the compounds, assailants may also have fired weapons to draw the attention of residents to window areas to maximize casualties.

The FBI and foreign partners have identified approximately 30 individuals thought to be involved in the planning and execution of the attack. Nearly all of these individuals have been killed or arrested by Saudi security forces.

AUGUST 5, 2003
Bombing of JW Marriott Hotel
Jakarta, Indonesia

On the afternoon of August 5, 2003, a vehicle-borne improvised explosive device (VBIED) exploded in front of the JW Marriott Hotel located in Mega Kuningan, South Jakarta, Indonesia. The blast killed 11 people, not including the suicide bomber, and injured 144 others, including two U.S. citizens. The blast caused extensive damage to the hotel and an adjacent office building.

Investigation by the Indonesian National Police, the Australian Federal Police, and the FBI traced responsibility for the bombing to Jemaah Islamiyah (JI), a transnational Southeast Asian terrorist organization based in Indonesia with close links to al-Qa'ida, which helped to finance the bombing.

The international investigation has identified over 30 individuals involved in the conspiracy to bomb the JW Marriott Hotel in Jakarta. Witness testimony has identified Noordin Mohammed Top as the leader of the operation and Dr. Azahari Husin as the bombmaker. Approximately 30 of the conspirators have been arrested, tried, and convicted in Indonesian courts and have received prison sentences ranging from three to 14 years. Husin was killed by Indonesian police during a shootout on November 9, 2005, in East Java, Indonesia. Top remained a fugitive at the end of 2005.

The investigation into the bombing of the JW Marriott Hotel in Jakarta is ongoing.

AUGUST 22, 2003
Vandalism and Destruction of Property
West Covina, California
(One act of Domestic Terrorism)

On August 22, 2003, individuals associated with the Earth Liberation Front (ELF) carried out acts of vandalism in the Los Angeles, California, area, damaging roughly 125 vehicles and one commercial building. Much of the damage was caused by spray-painted graffiti, although in two cases, individuals set fire to sport utility vehicles (SUVs). Some of the graffiti associated SUVs with "terrorism." On April 18, 2005, William Jensen Cottrell was sentenced to eight years and four months in federal prison and fined $3.5 million for the incident. Two other suspects in the attack—Tyler Johnson and Michie Oe—remained at large at the end of 2005.

AUGUST 28, 2003
Bombing
Emeryville, California
(One act of Domestic Terrorism)

On August 28, 2003, an improvised explosive device (IED) was detonated near the front door of Chiron Life Science Center in Emeryville, California, causing damage to the building. A second device detonated in another Chiron building shortly after first responders arrived at the scene, also damaging the building and the surrounding area. Chiron had previously received harassing e-mails, telephone calls, and faxes, and some Chiron employees had been harassed at their residences. Chiron, an animal testing laboratory, is associated with Huntingdon Life Sciences (HLS). HLS, and individuals and companies associated with it, have regularly been targeted by animal rights extremists. Daniel Andreas San Diego is suspected of having carried out the bombing and remained a fugitive at the end of 2005.

SEPTEMBER 26, 2003
Bombing
Pleasanton, California
(One act of Domestic Terrorism)

On September 26, 2003, an improvised explosive device was detonated at Shaklee Corporation in Pleasanton, California. Shaklee Corporation is a subsidiary of Yamanouchi Pharmaceutical Co. Ltd., which has been targeted by animal rights extremists in the past. Daniel Andreas San Diego is suspected of having carried out this bombing and the August 28, 2003, bombing at Chiron Life Science Center. San Diego remained a fugitive at the end of 2005.

2003 TERRORISM PREVENTIONS

FEBRUARY 13, 2003
Planned Attacks on Abortion Clinics and Minority Targets
Amwell Township, Pennsylvania
(Prevention of one act of Domestic Terrorism)

On February 13, 2003, law enforcement officials arrested David Wayne Hull, a long-time member and self-professed leader of the White Knights of the Ku Klux Klan (KKK). Hull had been exploding pipe bombs on his property in Amwell Township, Pennsylvania, had built and detonated improvised explosive devices (IEDs) during KKK events, and was recorded instructing individuals on how to place IEDs to cause maximum damage. Hull had also made threats against minorities and abortion clinics. Hull was indicted in March 2003 for firearms charges, witness tampering, and instructing persons on procedures for creating destructive devices. A jury in the Western District of Pennsylvania convicted Hull on seven counts of the ten-count indictment. On February 25, 2005, Hull was sentenced to 12 years in prison, followed by three years of probation.

APRIL 4, 2003
Planned Murder Plots against Federal Judge, AUSA, and IRS Agent
Grangeville, Idaho
(Prevention of one act of Domestic Terrorism)

On April 4, 2003, the FBI arrested David Roland Hinkson, a constitutionalist and tax protestor, for attempting to arrange the murders of a federal judge, an Assistant U.S. Attorney, and an IRS Agent whom he blamed for his legal problems regarding a tax evasion case against him. Between December 2002 and March 2003, Hinkson offered two individuals $10,000 for committing all three murders. On January 27, 2005, Hinkson was found guilty on three counts of solicitation to commit murder after a three week jury trial in Boise, Idaho. On June 3, 2005, Hinkson was sentenced to 43 years in federal prison.

APRIL 10, 2003
Planned Cyanide Attack
Tyler, Texas
(Prevention of one act of Domestic Terrorism)

On April 10, 2003, the FBI arrested William Joseph Krar for fraud-related charges stemming from his attempt to deliver numerous false identification badges—including a United Nations Observer Badges, Defense Intelligence Agency identification, and a Federal Concealed Weapons Permit—to Edward Feltus, a member of the New Jersey Militia. Krar had also been identified as a potential weapons supplier associated with extremist militia activities. In a search of Krar's Texas residence at the time of his arrest, FBI investigators found firearms, explosives, blasting caps, machine guns, over 100,000 rounds of ammunition, approximately 800 grams of sodium cyanide, and plans to weaponize the sodium cyanide. Krar and a co-conspirator, Judith Bruey, pled guilty to federal weapons charges, and in May 2004 were sentenced to 135 months and 57 months in federal custody, respectively. Feltus pled guilty to aiding and abetting the transportation of false IDs, and was sentenced in May 2004 to 18 months probation and fined $1,500.

JUNE 9, 2003
Planned Bombing of a U.S. Coast Guard Facility
Bellingham, Washington
(Prevention of one act of Domestic Terrorism)

On June 9, 2003, the FBI arrested Paul Douglas Revak for plotting to bomb a U.S. Coast Guard facility in Bellingham, Washington. Revak, who had previously declared himself to be an anarchist, was reportedly attempting to precipitate a revolution in the United States and had discussed the targeting of several nearby military installations. Revak was arrested when he negotiated with an undercover FBI employee for the purchase of explosive device components. Under a plea agreement, Revak was charged with threatening to use a weapon of mass destruction and sentenced to five years' probation.

NOVEMBER 11, 2003
Planned Bombings of Abortion Clinics
Miami, Florida
(Prevention of one act of Domestic Terrorism)

On November 11, 2003, Stephen John Jordi was arrested in Miami, Florida, for plotting to attack several abortion clinics. Jordi had openly discussed his intentions to attack abortion clinics, had expressed solidarity with anti-abortion extremists, and had associated with individuals from the anti-abortion extremist group Army of God. Jordi set out potential targets and a specific time frame for the attacks, and had cased and videotaped numerous Miami-area abortion clinics. He had also purchased several items to carry out the attack, including containers of gasoline and propane, flares, starting fluid, and a silencer purchased from an FBI source. Jordi was indicted on November 15, 2003, for attempting to damage and destroy property used in interstate commerce, distribution of information relating to the manufacture or use of explosive or destructive devices, and possession of a firearm that was not registered to him. On July 8, 2004, a federal judge in Miami sentenced Jordi to five years in prison.

2003 SIGNIFICANT EVENTS

JANUARY 30, 2003
Richard C. Reid Sentenced

On January 30, 2003, Richard Colvin Reid was sentenced to life in prison for his December 2001 attempt to bomb American Airlines flight 63 with an explosive device concealed in his shoe. Reid had been indicted on January 16, 2002, on nine terrorism-related counts, and pled guilty on October 4, 2002.

FEBRUARY 14, 2003
Kathleen Ann Soliah Sentenced

On February 14, 2003, Kathleen Ann Soliah, a former member of the Symbionese Liberation Army (SLA) serving time for her role in a 1975 car bombing plot, was sentenced for the 1975 murder of Myrna Opsahl. Soliah received six years added to the sentence she was already serving, after pleading guilty on November 7, 2002, for her role in the 1975 SLA bank robbery that killed Opsahl.

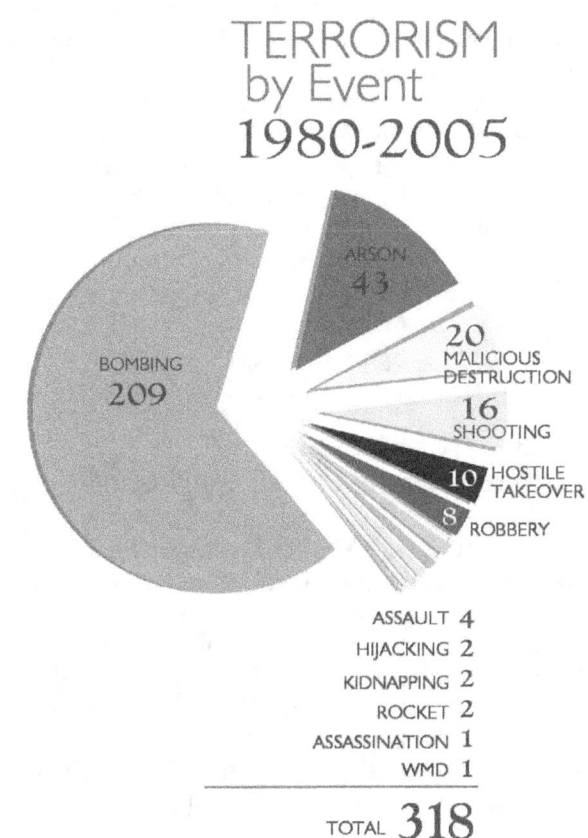

TERRORISM by Event 1980-2005

BOMBING 209
ARSON 43
20 MALICIOUS DESTRUCTION
16 SHOOTING
10 HOSTILE TAKEOVER
8 ROBBERY
ASSAULT 4
HIJACKING 2
KIDNAPPING 2
ROCKET 2
ASSASSINATION 1
WMD 1

TOTAL 318

FEBRUARY 19, 2003
Arrests and Indictments of Palestinian Islamic Jihad Members

On February 19, 2003, four members of the Palestinian Islamic Jihad (PIJ) terrorist organization—Sami Amin al-Arian, Sameeh Hammoudeh, Hatim Naji Fariz, and Ghassan Zayed Ballut — were arrested and charged with operating a racketeering enterprise from 1984 to 2003 in support of violence. The indictment, which was unsealed on February 20, 2003, also charged the individuals with "conspiracy within the United States to kill and maim persons abroad, conspiracy to provide material support and resources to PIJ, conspiracy to violate emergency economic sanctions," extortion, perjury, obstruction of justice, and immigration fraud. Four other individuals were also charged under the same indictment — Ramadan Abduallah Shallah, Bashir Musa Mohammed Nafi, Mohammed Tasir Hassan Al-Khatib, and Abd Al Aziz Awda — but were overseas and remained fugitives at the end of 2005.

FEBRUARY 28, 2003
Cigarette Smugglers Sentenced in Terror Financing Case

On February 28, 2003, Mohamad and Chawki Hammoud were sentenced to prison terms for their roles in a Charlotte, North Carolina-based, cigarette smuggling ring with ties to terrorist financing. Both men were convicted of cigarette smuggling, money laundering, racketeering, and credit card fraud. Mohamad Hammoud, who was found guilty of providing support to Hizballah in addition to smuggling charges, was given a maximum 155-year prison sentence. Chawki Hammoud, who was convicted in the smuggling case but was not found to have ties to Hizballah, was sentenced to 51 months in prison.

MARCH 1, 2003
Capture of Khalid Shaykh Mohammed

On March 1, 2003, counterterrorism forces in Pakistan captured Khalid Shaykh Mohammed, an al-Qa'ida operational commander and the man believed to have been the mastermind of the September 11, 2001, attack. Shaykh Mohammed is also believed to have played a role in a number of other attacks and planned attacks, including the 2002 bombings in Bali, Indonesia, the 2000 bombing of the USS Cole in Yemen, and a 1995 plot to blow up multiple U.S. commercial airliners.

APRIL 14, 2003
Plea Agreement for Earnest James Ujaama

On April 14, 2003, Earnest James Ujaama pled guilty in Seattle federal court to conspiring to provide goods and services to the Taliban in Afghanistan. As part of the plea agreement, federal prosecutors dropped charges alleging that Ujaama had plotted to establish a terrorist training camp in Bly, Oregon. In return, Ujaama was sentenced to 24 months in prison.

AUGUST 18, 2003
Sentencing of Enaam Arnaout

On August 18, 2003, Enaam Arnaout, the director of Benevolence International Foundation, was sentenced to 11 years in federal prison after pleading guilty on February 10, 2003, to terrorism-related racketeering conspiracy charges. Arnaout had been indicted on October 9, 2002, for conspiracy to fraudulently obtain charitable donations in order to provide financial assistance to al-Qa'ida and other organizations engaged in violence and terrorism. The indictment charged Arnaout with conspiracy to engage in racketeering, conspiracy to provide material support to terrorists, money laundering, mail fraud, and wire fraud in his attempt to fraudulently use the charitable contributions of Muslim Americans, U.S. corporations, and other donors to support terrorism overseas. Benevolence International Foundation was registered as a tax-exempt charitable organization; Arnaout allegedly used it as a racketeering enterprise.

AUGUST–DECEMBER 2003
Plea Agreements and Sentencing for Portland Terror Cell Suspects

Between August and December 2003, six of seven members of a Portland, Oregon-based terrorist cell pled guilty to terrorism-related charges. The six were indicted in October 2002 for conspiracy to provide assistance to Taliban and al-Qa'ida forces by planning to travel to fight U.S. troops stationed in Afghanistan. Charges against the seventh defendant, Habis Al Saoub, were dismissed after he was killed in Pakistan by Pakistani troops on October 3, 2003.

On August 6, 2003, Maher Hawash pled guilty to conspiracy to supply services to the Taliban. On September 18, 2003, brothers Ahmed and Muhammad Bilal pled guilty to federal weapons charges and conspiracy to contribute services to the Taliban. On September 26, 2003, October Martinique Lewis, the ex-wife of Jeffrey Leon Battle, pled guilty to money laundering for the purpose of assisting Battle in willfully supplying services to the Taliban. On October 16, 2003, Battle and Patrice Lumumba Ford pled guilty to seditious conspiracy. Prison sentences for cell members taken into custody ranged from three to 18 years.

OCTOBER 7, 2003
Sentencing of Raymond Anthony Sandoval

On October 7, 2003, a U.S. District judge in New Mexico sentenced Raymond Anthony Sandoval to 84 months incarceration and to make restitution payment of $3 million for having initiated the June 1998 Oso Complex wildfire near Espanola, New Mexico, and attempting to bomb the Santa Fe, New Mexico, offices of the Forest Guardians environmentalist group on March 19, 1999. On June 25, 2003, Sandoval pled guilty to charges of manufacturing a destructive device, possession of an unregistered firearm, arson on federal land, and willfully injuring property of the United States. Law enforcement officers with the FBI, U.S. Forest Service, and Espanola, New Mexico Police arrested Sandoval on February 14, 2003.

OCTOBER 28, 2003
Iyman Faris Sentenced for Material Support to al-Qa'ida

On October 28, 2003, a federal court in the Eastern District of Virginia sentenced U.S. citizen Iyman Faris (aka Mohammed Rauf) to 20 years in prison. Faris had been charged with conspiracy and providing material support to al-Qa'ida and pled guilty on May 1, 2003. According to the indictment and plea, Faris conducted casing of a New York City bridge and researched and provided information on U.S. targets to al-Qa'ida.

DECEMBER 2003
Sentencing of Lackawanna Six Terror Cell Members

In December 2003, Faysal Galab, Shafal Mosed, Yahya Goba, Sahim Alwan, Yasein Taher, and Mukhtar Albakri received federal prison sentences ranging from seven to 10 years after pleading guilty to providing material support or resources to al-Qa'ida. The six individuals, who resided in Lackawanna, New York, traveled to Afghanistan in the summer of 2001 to attend the al-Farooq terrorist training camp near Kandahar. Attendees were present at this camp for a period of up to two months and received terrorism training; several of the men were also present for a speech by Usama Bin Ladin. They were arrested in September of 2002 for providing material support or resources to a designated foreign terrorist organization.

2004 IN REVIEW

The FBI recorded five terrorist incidents and five terrorism preventions in 2004. Domestic extremists were responsible for each incident. Three of the incidents involved possible associates of the Earth Liberation Front environmental extremist movement, who used incendiary devices against car dealerships, construction sites and housing developments. In a fourth incident, associates of the Animal Liberation Front conducted two attacks against an animal science facility on the campus of Brigham Young University, which resulted in more than $75,000 in damages. Another incident involved a white supremacist affiliated with Aryan Nations who firebombed a synagogue in Oklahoma City, Oklahoma.

In the first terrorism prevention, law enforcement officers in Birmingham, Alabama, arrested two men in possession of multiple firearms, bomb-making literature, components of an improvised explosive device, and literature related to the Waco and Ruby Ridge incidents, as well as photographs of serial bomber Eric Rudolph. The second terrorism prevention involved the same white supremacist arrested in 2004 for firebombing an Oklahoma City synagogue, and for whom further investigation uncovered his intention to commit additional attacks against minorities. The third prevention involved a plot by extremist members of the Montana-based Project 7 Militia to kidnap and assassinate local judges, law enforcement officers, and their family members. The fourth prevention involved a Chicago-area man attempting to sell ammonium nitrate to an individual purportedly associated with a foreign terrorist organization. The fifth prevention involved the arrest of a man in Tennessee who wanted to obtain nuclear or chemical materials to blow up a courthouse.

No deaths or serious injuries resulted from terrorist activity carried out in the United States in 2004.

Among the major international terrorist incidents during 2004, al-Qa'ida conducted a series of terrorist attacks in Saudi Arabia against economic and diplomatic targets through kidnapings, murders, and suicide attacks using small groups of operatives. The attacks resulted in 36 deaths, including the deaths of six Americans, and over two dozen injuries, including those to four Americans. Another major incident involved the coordinated bombing of the train system in Madrid, Spain, by terrorists affiliated with the violent global jihadist movement. A total of 10 bombs detonated during the March 11 morning rush hour in Madrid, killing 191 persons and injuring more the 1,400. Although this incident did not result in any American casualties and is not elsewhere summarized in this report, the Madrid bombing is significant in showing the extension of global jihadist violence outside of predominantly Muslim nations.

2004 TERRORIST INCIDENTS

JANUARY 19, 2004
Arson
Henrico County, Virginia
(One act of Domestic Terrorism)

On January 19, 2004, Henrico County Fire Department officials discovered four Molotov cocktails that had been used to commit arson on a Ford car dealership. One Molotov cocktail scorched a vehicle in the dealership. Investigators on the scene also discovered a BMW on which the letters "XXX" were spray-painted. A business neighboring the dealership had the letters "XELFX" spray-painted on it. Christopher Kyle Salmon and Timothy Ryan Kennedy were convicted of attempted arson. Salmon was sentenced to 24 months in prison, two years of probation, and $500 restitution. Kennedy was sentenced to 25 months in prison, two years of probation, and $500 restitution.

APRIL 1, 2004
Arson
Oklahoma City, Oklahoma
(One act of Domestic Terrorism)

On April 1, 2004, Sean Michael Gillespie used a Molotov cocktail to firebomb the Temple B'nai Israel in Oklahoma City, Oklahoma. The attack caused mostly smoke damage to the synagogue. Gillespie committed the arson as a target of opportunity when he could not locate for a similar attack the address of a person he presumed to be Jewish, whose name he had randomly discovered in a phone book. On April 16, 2004, the FBI arrested Gillespie for the firebombing. A search of Gillespie's residence and truck revealed two videotapes, a baseball bat, brass knuckles, and a stun gun. One of the videotapes clearly implicates Gillespie in the firebombing of the synagogue. Gillespie had claimed association with the Aryan Nations and stated that he was proud of his actions. On April 26, 2005, Gillespie was convicted on charges related to the possession and use of an explosive device and on August 30, 2005, was sentenced to 39 years in prison.

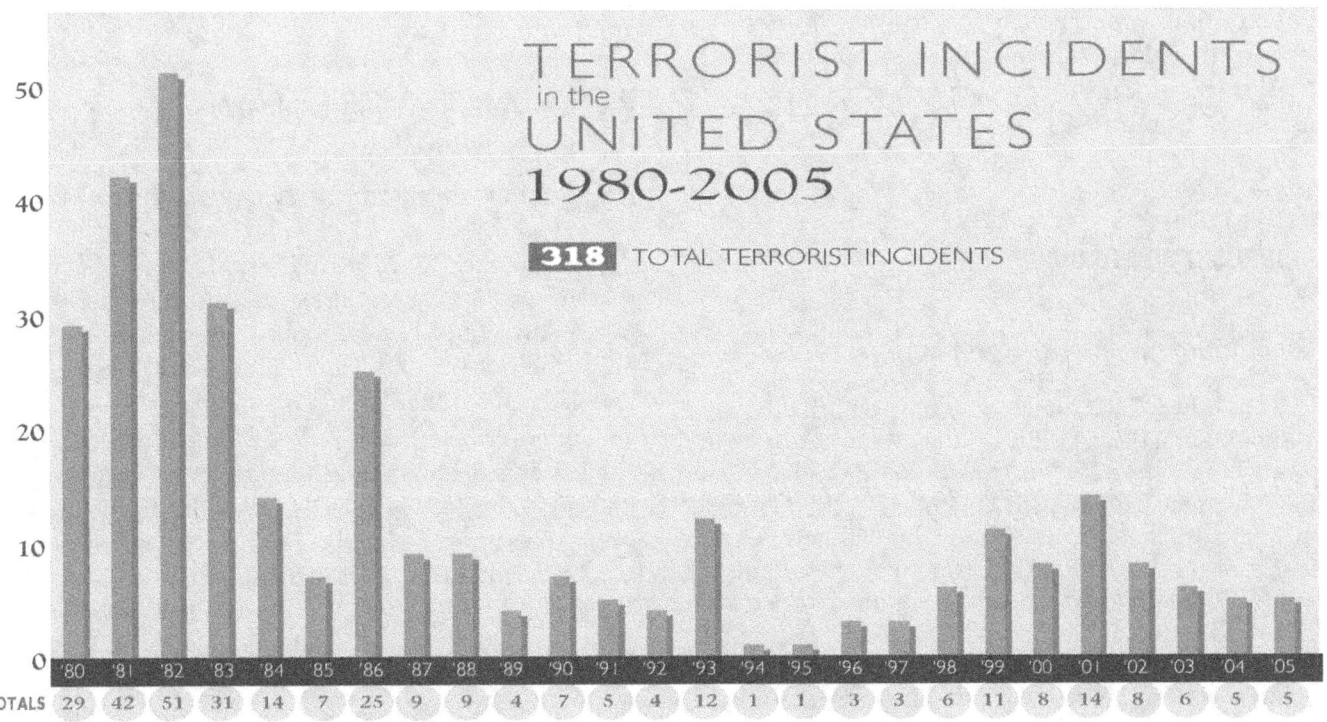

TERRORIST INCIDENTS in the UNITED STATES 1980-2005

318 TOTAL TERRORIST INCIDENTS

TOTALS	'80	'81	'82	'83	'84	'85	'86	'87	'88	'89	'90	'91	'92	'93	'94	'95	'96	'97	'98	'99	'00	'01	'02	'03	'04	'05
	29	42	51	31	14	7	25	9	9	4	7	5	4	12	1	1	3	3	6	11	8	14	8	6	5	5

APRIL 20, 2004
Vandalism and Arson
Snohomish, Washington
(One act of Domestic Terrorism)

In the early morning of April 20, 2004, two new homes were destroyed and another was damaged by arson, and an improvised incendiary device (IID) was found inside a fourth home at a new housing development in the Lobo Ridge area of Snohomish, Washington. The causes of the arson incidents are believed to be IIDs of the type recovered, consisting of jugs with duct-taped fuses and filled with flammable liquid. Approximately 20 miles away from the arson location, six containers of flammable liquid, duct tape, matches, and fuselike material were found by a contractor. The containers were found at the end of an uninhabited cul-de-sac of another new housing development along with graffiti that read "Consider these 13 as a warning. Walk on the edge. Green equals no burn all others are fair game. Bush is a rapist. ELF."

On April 21, 2004, three additional IIDs were found in a new construction subdivision several miles from where the previous day's incidents had occurred. The devices, which were ignited but failed to completely burn, resulted in no damage to the homes. The devices were similar to those found earlier. No note or claim of responsibility was found at this scene. The discovery of these three devices brought the total number of IIDs to 13, corresponding to the number warned of in the original ELF graffiti.

MAY - JULY, 2004
Vandalism and Arson
Provo, Utah
(One act of Domestic Terrorism)

On July 8, 2004, an arson occurred at the Ellsworth Farm animal science facility on the campus of Brigham Young University. The building was also vandalized and the walls spray painted with the phrases "ALF," "war is on," "you are the terrorists," and "this will never end." Damages from the fire and vandalism were estimated at over $75,000. Two related vandalism incidents attributed to the Animal Liberation Front (ALF) occurred at the same facility in May 2004. Harrison Burrows and Joshua Demmitt confessed to the July arson and May incidents. In January 2005 Burrows and Demmitt were each sentenced to 30 months in federal prison.

DECEMBER 27, 2004
Attempted Arson
Lincoln, California
(One act of Domestic Terrorism)

On December 27, 2004, four incendiary devices were placed in two homes under construction in Lincoln, California. However, the devices failed to function as intended. The site contained Earth Liberation Front (ELF)-related graffiti on one of the homes as well as the letters "ELF" on the cul-de-sac where the homes were located. Members of the Sacramento Joint Terrorism Task Force arrested Ryan Lewis, Eva Holland, Lili Holland, and Jeremiah Colcleasure in connection with the incident. The four were convicted of arson and Colcleasure, Holland, and Holland were each sentenced to two years in federal prison; Lewis received a six year prison sentence for his role in this incident and for arsons that took place in early 2005.

2004 TERRORISM PREVENTIONS

JANUARY 20, 2004
Planned Attacks Using Explosives
Birmingham, Alabama
(Prevention of one act of Domestic Terrorism)

On January 20, 2004, the Birmingham Joint Terrorism Task Force arrested David Nelson Hemphill for possession of pipe bombs and a homemade silencer. Subsequent searches of Hemphill's person and property revealed a .45-caliber handgun, bomb-making materials, antigovernment and bomb-making literature, and components of an ammonium nitrate fuel oil (ANFO) improvised explosive device. Hemphill admitted that prior to his arrest he had been trying to construct ANFO bombs. Hemphill's associate, Bruce Stephen Metzler, was also arrested. A search of Metzler's person and property revealed two .22-caliber handguns, a .233-caliber rifle, a .308-caliber assault rifle, a single- barrel shotgun, a .38-caliber revolver, literature related to the Waco and Ruby Ridge incidents, and photographs of an

Attacks by Al-Qa'ida in the Arabian Peninsula

Yanbu, Al Khobar, Riyadh, and Jeddah, Saudi Arabia

Early attacks by al-Qa'ida regional affiliate al-Qa'ida in the Arabian Peninsula (AQAP)—such as the May 12, 2003, coordinated bombings of three residential compounds in Riyadh, Saudi Arabia—focused on large mass-casualty events using vehicle-borne improvised explosive devices. After April 2004, AQAP changed tactics to include individual kidnapings, murders, and attacks against economic and diplomatic facilities using small teams of suicide operatives. Attacks by AQAP operatives that used these tactics and involved U.S. citizens or interests during 2004 include:

- On May 1, 2004, four gunmen drove into the ABB Lummus Global Compound at the Yanbu Petrochemical plant in Yanbu, Saudi Arabia. In the attack that followed, the assailants killed six ABB Lummus employees, including two Americans.
- On May 29, 2004, gunmen made a coordinated attack against Western and oil-infrastructure targets in Al Khobar, Saudi Arabia, including the Arab Petroleum Investments Corporation/Royal Dutch Shell compound, the Al Rushaid Petroleum Center, and the Oasis housing compound. The assailants killed 22 people in the attack, including one American, and wounded more than two dozen others, including four Americans.
- On June 8, 2004, gunmen fatally shot U.S. citizen Robert Corgan Jacobs, an employee of military training contractor Vinnell Arabia, as he walked from his car to his private residence in the al-Khalij section of Riyadh, Saudi Arabia.
- On June 12, 2004, three assailants fatally shot U.S. citizen Kenneth Raymond Scroggs as he returned from work to his residence in the Malaz District of Riyadh. Scroggs worked for Advanced Electronics, a Saudi business involved in the development of Apache Attack Helicopter systems.
- On June 12, 2004, U.S. citizen Paul Marshal Johnson, Jr., an employee of Advanced Electronics, was kidnaped in Riyadh. Johnson was killed by his captors six days later.
- On December 6, 2004, five armed assailants breached the U.S. consulate compound in Jeddah, Saudi Arabia. The terrorists were killed before gaining entrance to the consulate building. Five U.S. consulate Foreign Service Nationals died in the attack.

In response to these incidents, the FBI deployed investigative teams to assist Saudi authorities. Law enforcement actions have resulted in the deaths or capture of many of the perpetrators, including AQAP leader Abd al-Aziz al-Muqrin, who was killed in a shoot-out with Saudi authorities in June 2004.

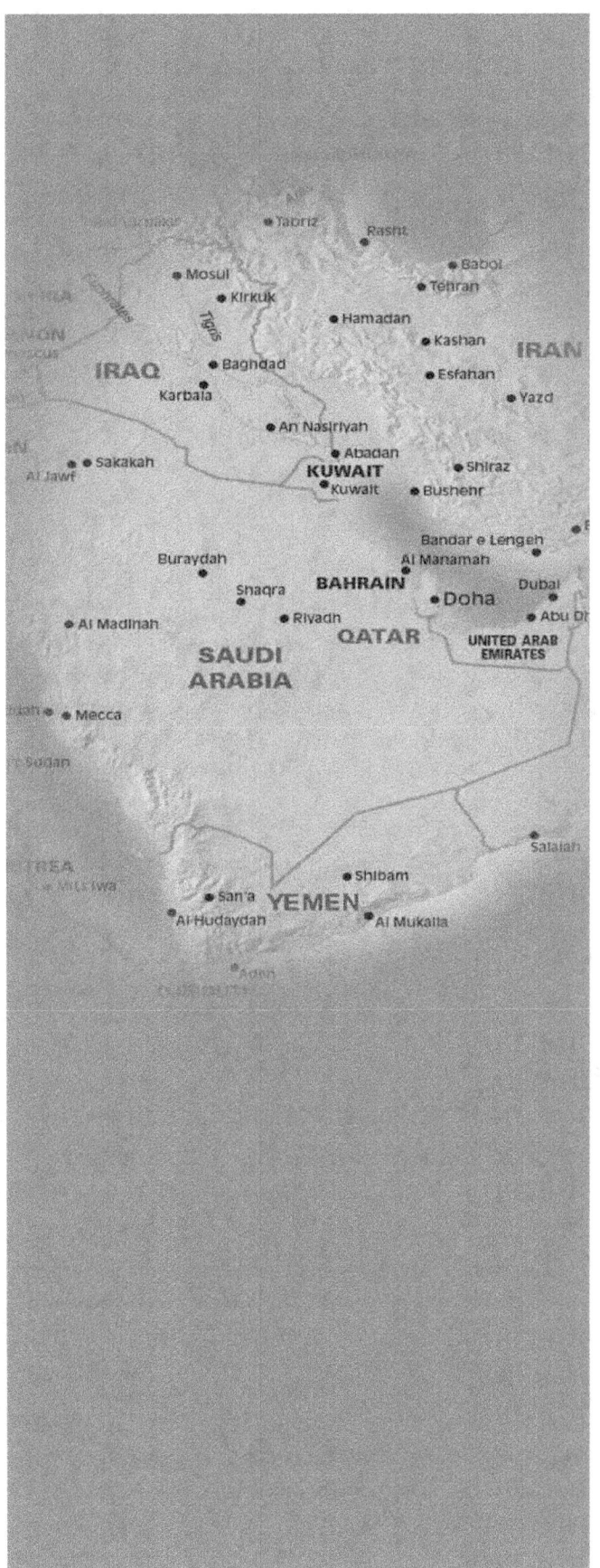

abortion clinic bombed by serial bomber Eric Rudolph. Also located were two empty 20 mm military ammunition containers, wire end caps, fuses, gunpowder, and a partially constructed silencer. Hemphill and Metzler pled guilty to weapons charges. On January 25, 2005, Hemphill was sentenced in the Southern District of Alabama to 23 months in prison followed by 24 months supervised release. On September 22, 2004, Metzler was sentenced to probation.

APRIL 16, 2004
Planned Attacks against Minorities
Oklahoma City, Oklahoma
(*Prevention of one act of Domestic Terrorism*)

As noted in 2004 Terrorist Incidents, the FBI arrested Sean Michael Gillespie on April 16, 2004, for having firebombed the Temple B'nai Israel in Oklahoma City, Oklahoma. The attack against the synagogue in Oklahoma City was likely the first of a series of unspecified attacks Gillespie intended to commit. Following Gillespie's arrest, a search of his residence revealed a videotape containing surveillance of a Las Vegas synagogue and a statement by Gillespie that he was on a "mission for the white race," which was to involve a cross-country spree of unspecified terrorist acts. Concern for future attacks was also supported by Gillespie's admission following his arrest to having previously committed random acts of vandalism and violence against minorities.

MAY 6, 2004
Convictions of Project 7 Militia Extremists
Flathead County, Montana
(*Prevention of one act of Domestic Terrorism*)

On May 6, 2004, several extremist members of the Project 7 Militia were arrested following an extensive investigation into the group by FBI, Bureau of Alcohol, Tobacco, and Firearms, and local police. Investigation had identified leader David Burgert and five other members of the Project 7 Militia as having committed various violations of federal law in furtherance of violent plans targeting law enforcement officers and other government officials. Burgert, along with Tracy Brockway, James Day, John Slater, and Steven Morey, pled guilty to

various federal weapons charges, including possession of machine guns and other illegal weapons as well as conspiracy to possess illegal weapons. On November 12, 2004, Burgert received an 87 month prison sentence for his role in the plotting. In early 2005, the four other members who entered guilty pleas received sentences ranging from 18 to 37 months in federal prison. A sixth subject, Larry Chezem, was convicted in a federal trial of conspiracy and was sentenced on September 30, 2005, to 15 months in prison.

AUGUST 5, 2004
Planned Attacks against Federal Buildings
Chicago, Illinois
(*Prevention of one act of Domestic Terrorism*)

On August 5, 2004, the FBI arrested Gale William Nettles in connection with his attempted sale of a half ton of ammonium nitrate to an undercover agent purportedly associated with a foreign terrorist organization. The FBI also had information that Nettles intended to use ammonium nitrate to bomb Chicago's Dirksen Federal Office Building. Nettles planned to counterfeit U.S. currency in order to earn money to purchase bomb components for his attack. On September 15, 2005, Nettles was found guilty of attempting to bomb the Dirksen Building and awaited sentencing at the end of 2005.

OCTOBER 25, 2004
Planned Attacks against Federal or State Courthouse
Memphis, Tennessee
(*Prevention of one act of Domestic Terrorism*)

On October 25, 2004, Demetrius Van Crocker was arrested in Jackson, Tennessee, for attempting to obtain C-4 explosives and Sarin nerve gas from an undercover FBI agent. Van Crocker was planning to use these materials to blow up a federal or state courthouse in furtherance of his hatred toward the U.S. and State of Tennessee governments. Van Crocker's federal trial on chemical weapons and explosives violations was pending at the end of 2005.

2004 SIGNIFICANT EVENTS

FEBRUARY 9, 2004
Final Sentencings in Portland Terror Cell Case

On February 9, 2004, three men affiliated with a terrorist cell in Portland, Oregon, were given prison sentences. Maher Hawash received a seven-year prison sentence, while two of his co-conspirators, Ahmed and Mohammed Bilal, were sentenced to ten and eight years in prison, respectively. The three men, along with three other suspects, pled guilty in 2003 to conspiracy to provide services to the Taliban and conspiracy to use firearms in a crime of violence. Several of these individuals had planned to travel to Afghanistan to fight alongside the Taliban against U.S. and Coalition forces. Three other Portland cell members were sentenced in 2003.

MARCH THROUGH APRIL 2004
"Virginia Jihad" Members Convicted and Sentenced

On April 9, 2004, Randall T. Royer and Ibrahim Ahmed al-Hamdi were sentenced to 20 years and 15 years in prison, respectively, for their roles in an alleged "Virginia Jihad" terrorist cell, which conducted weapons training in Virginia. On March 4, 2004, Masoud Khan, Seifullah Chapman, and Hammad Abdur-Raheem, three other cell members arrested in the case, were convicted on conspiracy and weapons charges. Two other men, Yong Ki Kwon and Khwarja Mahmood Hasan, pled guilty in the case, and testified that they had attended a training camp associated with the terrorist group Lashkar-e-Tayyiba with the intention of fighting on the side of the Taliban against U.S. forces in Afghanistan. The remaining two members of the group were not convicted. A federal judge acquitted Sabri Benkhala on March 9, 2004, and the case against Caliph Basha Ibn Abdur-Raheem was dismissed.

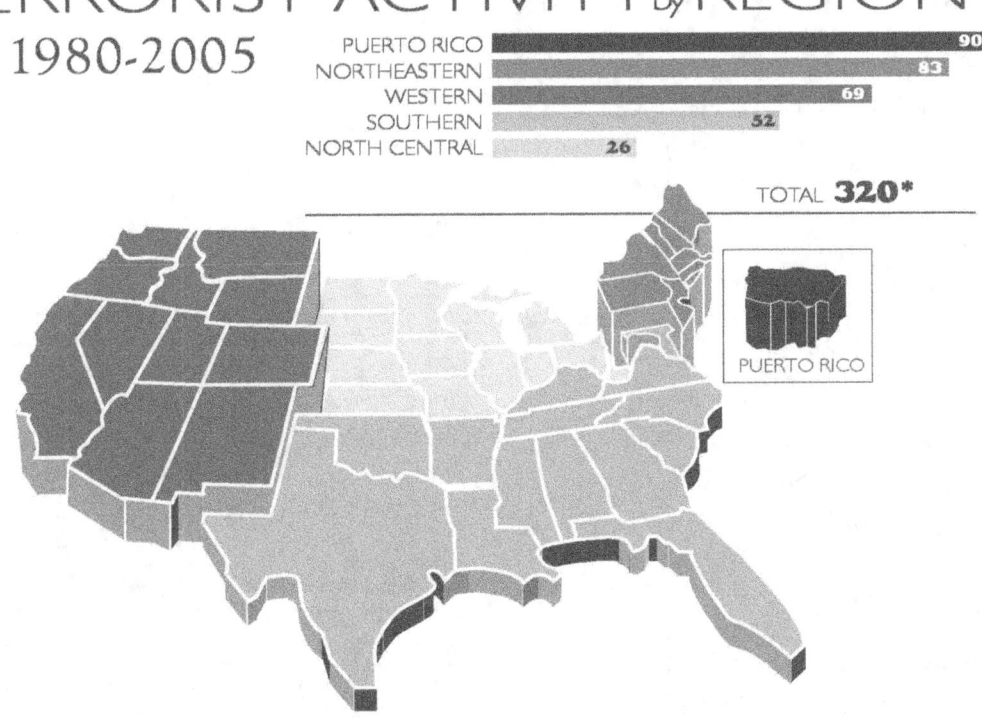

TERRORIST ACTIVITY by REGION
1980-2005

PUERTO RICO 90
NORTHEASTERN 83
WESTERN 69
SOUTHERN 52
NORTH CENTRAL 26

TOTAL **320***

PUERTO RICO

* Although designated as a single act of international terrorism, the aircraft attacks of September 11, 2001, have been designated as one terrorist incident in the Northeastern region and one terrorist incident in the Southern region for the purposes of this graph. Similarly, although the anthrax mailings that occurred from September through November 2001 have been categorized as a single act of terrorism, the incidents have been designated as one terrorist incident in the Northeastern region and one terrorist incident in the Southern region for the purposes of this graph.

APRIL 26, 2004
Sentencing of Symbionese Liberation Army Member

On April 26, 2004, Symbionese Liberation Army (SLA) member James William Kilgore was sentenced to 48 months in prison for several bombings in California in 1975. Kilgore was also sentenced to six months in prison for passport fraud charges. Kilgore was arrested in Cape Town, South Africa, in 2002 and was indicted for multiple murders, possession of an explosives device, and other charges in conjunction with his membership in the SLA, an organization that sought to overthrow the U.S. government in the 1970s.

JUNE 2, 2004
Mohammed Junaid Babar Guilty Plea

On April 10, 2004, the FBI arrested naturalized U.S. citizen Mohammed Junaid Babar in New York City for his suspected role in providing material support to al-Qa'ida that included support for a terrorist plot to blow up pubs, train stations, and restaurants in the United Kingdom. This arrest followed police actions by British authorities, who, in late March 2004, arrested eight British citizens and seized approximately 1,320 pounds of ammonium nitrate from a self-storage warehouse in west London in connection with the same plot. On June 2, 2004, Junaid Babar pled guilty in the Southern District of New York to five counts of conspiring to provide material support to al-Qa'ida. Sentencing for Junaid Babar was pending at the end of 2005.

JUNE 10, 2004
Nuradin M. Abdi Indicted

On June 10, 2004, a federal grand jury indicted Nuradin M. Abdi on terrorism charges. The four-count indictment included charges of conspiracy to provide material support to terrorists; conspiracy to provide material support to al Qa'ida, a designated foreign terrorist organization; fraud and misuse of documents; and fraudulent use of travel documents. Abdi, a Somali national living in the United States, is believed to have misrepresented his reasons for travel on a federal govern-

ment form, claiming he intended to travel to Germany and Saudi Arabia for religious and family reasons when he actually planned to travel to Ethiopia for terrorism training. Abdi allegedly conspired to blow up a shopping mall in the Columbus, Ohio, area and engaged in explosives instruction in preparation for this plot. Abdi is also accused of obtaining refugee asylum status through false means. The indictment was originally filed under seal and was unsealed on June 14, 2005.

JULY 26, 2004
The 9/11 Commission Report Published

On July 26, 2004, the National Commission on Terrorist Attacks Upon the United States issued its final report on the September 11, 2001, attack. The report accounted for the circumstances surrounding the attack and provided recommendations for change. The FBI had submitted to the commission the "Report to the National Commission on Terrorist Attacks Upon the United States: The FBI's Counterterrorism Program Since September 2001" on April 14, 2004. This report covers the FBI's efforts to improve its counterterrorism capabilities since the attacks of September 11 and supplemented the testimony of several senior FBI officials.

AUGUST 19, 2004
Indictment of HAMAS Associates for Criminal Enterprise

On August 19, 2004, the FBI arrested Muhammad Salah, of Chicago, and Abdelhaleem Ashqar, of Washington, D.C., and issued an arrest warrant for Mousa Abu Marzook, a former U.S. resident who currently resides in Damascus, Syria, and is considered to be a fugitive from justice. These arrest actions followed an indictment by a federal grand jury in Chicago that alleged the three participated in a 15-year racketeering conspiracy in the United States and abroad by joining with 20 identified co-conspirators and others in illegally conducting the affairs of the foreign terrorist organization HAMAS. The indictment, which for the first time identifies HAMAS as a criminal enterprise, alleges that Salah, Ashqar, and Marzook provided money and personnel to HAMAS at a time when HAMAS was engaging in terrorist attacks. Although the defendants were not charged with direct participation in violence, these attacks resulted in the deaths of Israeli military personnel and civilians, as well as American and other foreign nationals in Israel and the West Bank. Trial for the defendants was pending at the end of 2005.

SEPTEMBER 22, 2004
Nevada Chapter Leader of Aryan Nations Arrested for Sending Threatening Letters

In December 2003, Steven Joseph Holten, the Nevada Chapter leader for Aryan Nations (AN), began a letter-writing campaign announcing the existence of AN in Nevada and condemning the actions of certain federal, media, and Jewish institutions. Many of the letters contained specific threats to the recipients. On September 22, 2004, FBI agents in Reno arrested Holten. On November 29, 2004, Holten pled guilty to mailing threatening communications through interstate commerce. On March 28, 2005, Holten was sentenced to ten months in prison, three years of supervised release, and a mandatory $100 fine.

SEPTEMBER 29, 2004
Sentencings in *USS Cole* Bombing

On September 29, 2004, a Yemeni court sentenced Abd al-Rahim al-Nashiri and Jamal al-Badawi to death for their roles in the October 12, 2000, bombing of the *USS Cole* in the Port of Aden, Yemen. Four other men were given prison sentences, ranging from five to 10 years, for their roles in the attack. Seventeen American sailors were killed and more than 40 were injured in the October 12, 2000 bombing of the *USS Cole*, in which two suicide terrorists pulled a small, bomb-laden boat alongside the U.S. destroyer and detonated their explosives. Al-Badawi was also charged with a similar, failed attack against the *USS The Sullivans* in January 2000.

DECEMBER 8, 2004
Signing of the Intelligence Reform and Terrorism Prevention Act of 2004

On December 8, 2004, President Bush signed into law the Intelligence Reform and Terrorism Prevention Act of 2004 (IRTPA). In direct response to the recom-

mendations of the 9/11 Commission, IRTPA instituted reforms to the Foreign Intelligence Surveillance Act and modified material support statutes for prosecuting terrorists. Among its many organizational provisions, IRTPA created the Office of the Director of National Intelligence; established the Director of National Intelligence as the head of the U.S. Intelligence Community; and instituted the joint-agency National Counterterrorism Center as the primary entity for analyzing intelligence pertaining to transnational terrorism.

DECEMBER 13, 2004
Yemeni Terror Suspects Indicted

On December 13, 2004, a federal grand jury in the Eastern District of New York indicted two Yemeni nationals, Sheik Mohammad Ali Hassan Al-Moayad and Mohammed Mohsen Yahya Zayed, for conspiracy and attempt to provide material support to al-Qa'ida and HAMAS. Al-Moayad allegedly supported *mujahideen* around the world, and is believed to have provided money and equipment to al-Qa'ida and raised funds through a Brooklyn mosque for terrorism financing.

I n 2005, the FBI recorded five terrorist incidents and three terrorism preventions. All of the incidents involved arson or attempted arson. Domestic terrorists associated with the Earth Liberation Front were responsible for three of the incidents, which targeted commercial and residential construction sites. The other two incidents targeted the residences of persons involved with animal research. One of these incidents was claimed by the Animal Liberation Front, and the other is possibly attributable to animal rights extremists as well.

Separate preventions in Houston, Texas, and Pocatello, Idaho, involved individuals who sought to provide material support or resources to al-Qa'ida. A third prevention involved a group that formed in a Los Angeles prison, which adopted a jihadist ideology and was preparing to commit terrorist acts in the United States in furtherance of the violent global jihadist movement.

No deaths or serious injuries resulted from terrorist activity carried out in the United States in 2005.

A major international terrorist incident in 2005 involved the coordinated suicide bombing of the transit system in London, United Kingdom. The attack, carried out by British citizens affiliated with the violent global jihadist movement, resulted in 52 deaths and approximately 700 injuries. One American died in the attack and four others were injured.

2005 TERRORIST INCIDENTS

JANUARY – FEBRUARY 2005
Arson and Attempted Arson
Auburn and Sutter Creek, California
(One act of Domestic Terrorism)

On January 12, 2005, five intact incendiary devices were discovered at a commercial construc-
tion site in Auburn, California. On January 21, 2005, a letter was sent to four newspapers claiming responsibility for the attempted arson by the Earth Liberation Front (ELF).

On February 7, 2005, an arson was reported at an apartment complex in Sutter Creek, California. Fire officials discovered seven partially burned incendiary devices placed in five buildings of the apartment complex. Graffiti found at the site included "ELF" and "We Will Win" in red paint. Sprinkler systems installed in the buildings extinguished six of the seven devices and first responders extinguished the seventh. Damage was estimated at $50,000.

Ryan Daniel Lewis was convicted of arson and attempted arson involving these collective incidents as well as a December 27, 2004, incident in Lincoln, California. On March 17, 2005, Lewis was sentenced to a 72-month prison term followed by three years of supervised release.

JULY 7, 2005
Bombing of London Transportation System
London, United Kingdom

On July 7, 2005, a series of coordinated suicide bomb blasts struck London's transport system during morning rush hour. Beginning at 8:50 a.m. three bombs exploded within 50 seconds of each other on three London Underground trains, and a fourth bomb exploded on a bus nearly an hour later at 9:47 a.m. in London's Tavistock Square. Fifty-two people were killed and approximately 700 injured in the bombing. Among the casualties were one American killed and four wounded.

The four suicide bombers were British citizens; three had been born in the United Kingdom, and the fourth had been born in Jamaica. The British citizenship of the bombers and the lack of strong ties between them and an international terrorist group illustrate the potential threat of "homegrown" terrorists as perpetrators of future attacks.

APRIL 13, 2005
Arson
Sammamish, Washington
(One act of Domestic Terrorism)

In the early morning of April 13, 2005, arson occurred at a nearly completed residence under construction in Sammamish, Washington, and an intact improvised incendiary device (IID) was discovered in a second residence under construction nearby. The IID in the first residence was located in the garage, which was destroyed by the fire. The second IID — a plastic, two-liter bottle filled with fuel and using an improvised igniter — had been placed under debris in the kitchen nook. The device had been activated but did not fully ignite. In addition a bedsheet with the wording, "Where are all the trees? Burn rapist burn. ELF," had been placed outside the second residence.

JULY 7, 2005
Attempted Arson
Los Angeles, California
(One act of Domestic Terrorism)

In the early morning of July 7, 2005, fire officials responded to a vehicle fire in the driveway of a private residence in Los Angeles, California. In extinguishing the fire, authorities recovered a partially melted, plastic gasoline container from behind the vehicle's left front wheel. The car belonged to a representative for the Animal Care Technicians Union, which represents employees for the Los Angeles Animal Services (LAAS). LAAS and its affiliates have been targeted by local animal rights extremists, and the LAAS union representative had been placed on a "targets" list of individuals profiled by extremists for "direct actions." The incident remains under investigation.

SEPTEMBER 16, 2005
Attempted Arson
Los Angeles, California
(*One act of Domestic Terrorism*)

On September 16, 2005, fire officials responded to a fire at the high-rise condominium home of the director of Los Angeles Animal Services, after residents observed smoke coming from a recyclables/janitorial closet. First responders recovered an improvised incendiary device consisting of a four-inch-long tube labeled "TOXIC" and using a cigarette as a fuse. The device, which had been placed next to a stack of newspapers in the recycling/janitorial closet, had malfunctioned and only scorched the concrete floor of the closet. The Animal Liberation Front claimed responsibility for this incident.

NOVEMBER 20, 2005
Arson
Hagerstown, Maryland
(*One act of Domestic Terrorism*)

In the early morning of November 20, 2005, five townhomes under construction were set on fire at the Hagers Crossing Development in Hagerstown, Maryland. Fire officials investigating the scene determined that kerosene was used as the accelerant in the arson. The blaze damaged or destroyed five units in two buildings. The Earth Liberation Front claimed responsibility for the fire.

OCTOBER 1, 2005
Kuta and Jimbaran Bombings
Bali, Indonesia

On October 1, 2005, three suicide bombers affiliated with the Jemaah Islamiya (JI) terrorist organization used improvised explosive devices to conduct attacks against targets in the towns of Kutu and Jimbaran, outside the provincial capital of Denpasar, on the island of Bali, Indonesia. The bombers, who either wore vests or carried backpacks containing the explosives, targeted the Raja Restaurant in Kuta Square, the Nyoman Café in Jimbaran Beach, and the Mandega Café also in Jimbaran Beach and located across from the Four Seasons and Intercontinental Hotels.

The bombings killed 22 persons and injured 102. The FBI reported that those injured included a family of six U.S. and Indonesian dual national individuals, who were dining at the Raja Restaurant in Kuta.

On November 9, 2005, officers from the Indonesian National Police, working on leads from the October 1st bombing, conducted a number of law enforcement operations throughout the island of Java, Indonesia. These operations resulted in the arrests of a number of JI associates and the death of JI bomb-maker Azahari Husin. Husin was one of the most wanted terrorists in Southeast Asia and was a suspect in both the Kuta and Jimbaran bombing operation and the October 12, 2002, bombing of a Balinese nightclub.

2005 TERRORISM PREVENTIONS

MAY 20, 2005
Attempt to Build and Sell Explosives
Houston, Texas
(Prevention of one act of Terrorism)

On May 20, 2005, FBI Special Agents arrested Ronald Allen Grecula following an arranged meeting with undercover officers. During the meeting, Grecula presented his design for a bomb, which he allegedly understood would be used by al-Qa'ida to kill Americans. On June 16, 2005, the U.S. District Court, Southern District of Texas, indicted Grecula on one count of providing material support or resources to a designated foreign terrorist organization. The indictment stemmed from information that indicated Grecula intended to build and sell a bomb to a terrorist organization for use against the United States.

JULY 5, 2005
Disruption of Plot to Attack Military and Jewish Targets
Los Angeles County, California
(Prevention of one act of International Terrorism)

On July 5, 2005, officers with the Torrance (California) Police Department arrested Levar Washington and Gregory Patterson during a commercial armed robbery in progress at a Los Angeles area gas station. Their arrest, and subsequent local and FBI investigation, revealed that Washington and Patterson were conducting the armed robberies to raise money for an alleged terrorist plot targeting U.S. military facilities, Israeli government facilities, and Jewish synagogues in the greater Los Angeles area. FBI investigation determined that Washington and Patterson were part of a Muslim convert organization, Jam'iyyat Ul-Islam Is-Saheeh ("Authentic Assembly of Islam"), or JIS, allegedly founded in prison by inmate Kevin James in 1997. The FBI identified James, Washington, Patterson—all U.S. citizens—and Hammad Samana, a Permanent Resident Alien of Pakistani origin, as the primary members of JIS. Samana was arrested on August 1, 2005.

On August 31, 2005, a federal grand jury in Santa Ana, California, indicted James, Washington, Patterson, and Samana for their alleged roles in the terrorist plot on charges of conspiracy to levy war against the U.S. government through terrorism and conspiracy to possess and discharge firearms in furtherance of crimes of violence. Washington, Patterson, and Samana were also charged with conspiracy to kill members of the U.S. government uniformed services and conspiracy to kill foreign officials. Washington and Patterson were further charged with interference with commerce by robbery and using and carrying a firearm in connection with a crime of violence.

DECEMBER 5, 2005
Planned Attacks Against Pipeline Systems
Pocatello, Idaho
(Prevention of one act of International Terrorism)

On December 5, 2005, Michael Curtis Reynolds was arrested at a motel near Pocatello, Idaho, after arranging to meet a purported al-Qa'ida contact. Reynolds offered to assist al-Qa'ida in engaging in acts of terrorism within the United States by identifying targets, planning terrorist attacks, and describing bomb-making methods. Reynolds sought to carry out violent attacks against pipeline systems and energy facilities in an effort to reduce energy reserves, create environmental hazards, and increase anxiety. Reynolds sought payment for supplying his assistance and continuing work on behalf of al-Qa'ida. Reynolds has been charged with attempting to provide material support to a foreign terrorist organization.

2005 SIGNIFICANT EVENTS

FEBRUARY 10, 2005
Associates of Imprisoned Sheikh Convicted

On February 10, 2005, a federal jury in Manhattan convicted Lynne Stewart, an attorney representing Sheik Omar Abdul Rahman the "Blind Sheikh"; Mohammed Yousry, a translator for Rahman's attorneys; and Ahmed Abdel Sattar, a follower of Rahman in New York, on charges including providing and concealing the provision of material support or resources to terrorists. Rahman, who was convicted of a 1993 conspiracy to bomb several New York City landmarks, is the spiritual leader of the Egyptian-based terrorist organization Al-Gama Al-Islamiya.

FEBRUARY 17, 2005
Indictment against the Al-Haramain Islamic Foundation

On February 17, 2005, a federal grand jury returned a three-count indictment against the Ashland, Oregon-based Al-Haramain Islamic Foundation, Inc., and two of its officers on charges of conspiring to defraud the U.S. government and concealing their intent by filing a false tax return and failing to acknowledge they were transporting funds out of the United States. The charges of conspiracy to defraud the United States, tax fraud, and currency smuggling revolve around a $150,000 transaction apparently intended for the benefit of Chechen *mujahideen.*

MARCH 1, 2005
Kourani Pleads Guilty

On March 1, 2005, Mahmoud Youssef Kourani pled guilty to one count of conspiracy to provide material support to the designated foreign terrorist organization Hizballah. The guilty plea came in response to meetings Kourani hosted at his home, during which a guest speaker from Lebanon solicited donations to Hizballah's "orphans of martyrs" program to benefit the families of Hizballah members killed in action. Kourani was sentenced on June 14, 2005, to a 54-month prison term to be followed by his removal upon release.

MARCH 10, 2005
Al-Moayed and Zayed Convicted

On March 10, 2005, a federal jury convicted Yemeni cleric Mohamed Al-Moayed and Mohammed Zayed on charges of providing and conspiring to provide material support and resources to al-Qa'ida and HAMAS. Tape-recorded statements from Al-Moayad indicated that he was engaged in providing money to support *mujahideen* fighters in Afghanistan, Chechnya, and Kashmir. Al-Moayed and Zayed were arrested in Germany in January 2003 and charged with providing, and conspiring to provide, material support to terrorism. On July 28, 2005, Al-Moayed was sentenced to a 75-year prison term; Zayed was sentenced to a 45-year prison term.

APRIL 6, 2005
Hale Sentenced

On April 6, 2005, Matthew Hale, leader of the white supremacist Creativity Movement was sentenced to 40 years in prison. Hale had been convicted on three counts of obstruction of justice and soliciting the murder of Joan Lefkow, a federal judge in Chicago. Hale was arrested on January 8, 2003, for attempting to arrange the murder of Judge Lefkow, who had previously upheld a ruling against Hale in a trademark infringement case.

APRIL 13, 2005
Elashi Brothers Convicted

On April 13, 2005, a federal jury convicted Bayan Elashi, Basman Elashi, Ghassan Elashi, and the Infocom Corporation of conspiring and sending money to co-defendant Mousa Abu Marzook, an investor in Infocom and a self-admitted leader of HAMAS. In 1995, the U.S. Department of Treasury named HAMAS a specially designated terrorist organization, making it illegal for any U.S. person or entity to conduct business with HAMAS or its representatives.

APRIL 22, 2005
Guilty Plea of Zacarias Moussaoui

On April 22, 2005, Zacarias Moussaoui pled guilty to six charges related to his participation in the 9/11 conspiracy. Moussaoui admitted he had trained with al-Qa'ida in Afghanistan; had communicated directly with Usama Bin Ladin; and had been personally selected by Bin Ladin to participate in an operation to fly hijacked airplanes into American buildings, and who approved him to attack the White House.

APRIL 26, 2005
Ali Al-Timimi Convicted

On April 26, 2005, Ali Al-Timimi was convicted on all charges brought against him in connection with the "Virginia Jihad" case. Al-Timimi, a spiritual leader at a mosque in Northern Virginia, encouraged other individuals to go to Pakistan to receive military training from Lashkar-e-Tayyiba, a designated foreign terrorist organization, in order to fight U.S. troops in Afghanistan. Al-Timimi was sentenced to life in prison.

APRIL 27, 2005
Hemant Lakhani Convicted

On April 27, 2005, a federal jury in the District of New Jersey convicted British national Hemant Lakhani on charges of attempting to sell shoulder-fired missiles to what he thought was a terrorist group intent on shooting down U.S. airliners. Lakhani was arrested following an undercover sting operation involving agents from several nations. Lakhani was sentenced on September 11, 2005, to 47 years in prison.

JULY 7, 2005
Clayton Lee Waagner Sentenced

On July 7, 2005, anti-abortion extremist Clayton Lee Waagner was sentenced in the Southern District of Ohio to 19 years in federal prison for acts of violence he committed against abortion clinics in 2003 and for sending hoax anthrax letters to several reproductive health clinics in 2001.

JULY 18, 2005
Rudolph Sentenced

On July 18, 2005, a federal judge in Birmingham, Alabama, sentenced convicted bomber Eric Robert Rudolph to life in prison for the 1998 bombing of a Birmingham family planning clinic that killed a police officer and critically injured a nurse. On May 31, 2003, Rudolph had been arrested and charged with the clinic bombing as well as the bombing of Centennial Olympic Park in Atlanta, Georgia, two bombings at the Sandy Springs Professional Office Building near Atlanta, and two bombings at the Otherside Lounge in Atlanta. Rudolph pled guilty to the charges in April 2005.

JULY 26, 2005
Aref Ahmed Sentenced

On July 26, 2005, a federal judge in Buffalo, New York, sentenced Yemeni-American businessman Aref Ahmed to three years' imprisonment for his role in a cigarette-smuggling operation that may have been linked to terrorist activity. According to federal prosecutors, Ahmed gave $14,000 to five members of the Lackawanna Six to facilitate their travel to and attendance at a terrorist training camp. Members of the Lackawanna Six were charged with conspiring, providing, and attempting to provide material support to al-Qa'ida based upon their travel to Afghanistan to train in the al-Farooq camp operated by al-Qa'ida.

JULY 27, 2005
Ressam Sentenced

On July 27, 2005, Ahmed Ressam was sentenced to 22 years in prison for conspiracy to commit an international terrorist act and smuggling explosives. Ressam had been arrested on December 14, 1999, in Port Angeles, Washington, as he attempted to smuggle explosives into the United States for use in the Millennium Bombing plot against Los Angeles International Airport.

AUGUST 8, 2005
Carlos E. Gamarra-Murillo Sentenced

On August 8, 2005, Carlos Gamarra-Murillo was sentenced in U.S. District Court in Tampa, Florida, to 25 years' imprisonment for brokering and exporting defense articles without a license and providing material support to a foreign terrorist organization. Gamarra-Murillo attempted to supply the Colombian-based FARC with 4,000 grenades and 200 firearms.

AUGUST 25, 2005
Qureshi Sentenced

On August 25, 2005, Mohammed Salman Farooq Qureshi was sentenced in the Western District of Louisiana to four years of federal incarceration. On February 11, 2005, Qureshi pled guilty to making false statements to the FBI and provided information that established Qureshi's connections to and contacts with al-Qa'ida member Wadih El Hage. In addition, Qureshi provided information about his activities and financial support of the nongovernmental organization Help Africa People, which was believed to have been used by El Hage and others in connection with the attacks on the U.S. embassies in Kenya and Tanzania.

NOVEMBER 8, 2005
Young Sentenced

On November 8, 2005, a federal judge in Madison, Wisconsin, sentenced Peter Daniel Young to 24 months in prison following his September 2, 2005, guilty plea to one count of conspiracy and one count of animal enterprise terrorism. Young and Justin C. Samuel had been indicted by a grand jury for actions in releasing thousands of mink from three Wisconsin farms in late 1997. Samuel was extradited from Belgium and later pled guilty to two counts of animal enterprise terrorism on November 3, 2000. Young remained a federal fugitive until his capture by the San Jose Police Department in San Jose, California, on March 21, 2005.

NOVEMBER 22, 2005
Jose Padilla Indicted

On November 22, 2005, a federal grand jury in Miami, Florida, indicted Jose Padilla on charges of conspiring to "murder, kidnap and maim persons" overseas and providing material support to terrorists as part of a North American terrorist support cell. Padilla was arrested in Chicago on May 8, 2002. He allegedly trained with al-Qa'ida while on travel in Afghanistan and Pakistan during 2001.

NOVEMBER 22, 2005
Ahmad Abu Ali Convicted of Terrorist Plots

On November 22, 2005, a federal jury in the Eastern District of Virginia convicted Ahmad Abu Ali on all counts of an indictment charging him with terrorism offenses of providing material support and resources to al-Qa'ida and conspiracy to commit air piracy and conspiracy to destroy aircraft. An investigation revealed that Ali had sought out and joined an al-Qai'da cell in Medina, Saudi Arabia, where he received training in weapons, explosives, and document forgery. He, along with other members of the cell, began to develop plans for several terrorist attacks against the United States, including a plot to assassinate President Bush.

NOVEMBER 23, 2005
Paracha Convicted

On November 23, 2005, a federal jury in the Southern District of New York convicted Uzair Paracha, a Pakistani national with permanent resident alien status in the United States, on charges of providing material support to al-Qa'ida. Evidence at trial proved that Paracha agreed with his father, Saifullah Paracha, and al-Qa'ida members Majid Kahn and Ammar Al-Baluchi to provide material support to al-Qa'ida by trying to help Kahn reenter the United States to commit a terrorist act. The elder Paracha was in custody at the U.S. military prison in Guantanamo Bay, Cuba, at the end of 2005.

DECEMBER 5, 2005
"Operation Backfire" Arrests

On December 7, 2005, the following individuals were taken into federal custody on arson charges stemming from a series of approximately 25 criminal actions that occurred from 1996 to 2001 in a major investigation collectively referred to as Operation Backfire: Stanislas Meyerhoff (Charlottesville, Virginia), Kevin Tubbs (Springfield, Oregon), Daniel McGowan (New York, New York), Chelsea Gerlach (Portland, Oregon), Sarah Kendall Harvey (Flagstaff, Arizona), and William Rodgers (Prescott, Arizona). Rodgers later committed suicide while in state custody on December 22, 2005. Meyerhoff and McGowan were also charged with multiple counts of use of an incendiary device. Darren Thurston, a Canadian citizen, was arrested on immigration charges in connection with the case. In addition, Grand Jury subpoenas were issued to Jennifer Adrian, Joseph Dibee, Frank Winbigler, Shannon Urich, Suzanne Savoie, Jonathan Paul, and Jennifer Kolar. The location of Dibee and another suspect, Josephine Overaker, were unknown at the end of 2005.

The subjects of the Backfire investigation are suspected of having committed a series of arsons in Oregon, Washington, Colorado, Wyoming, and California on behalf of the Animal Liberation Front and Earth Liberation Front. Among the most significant of these actions were the October 19, 1998, Vail Ski Resort arson in Vail, Colorado, that resulted in an estimated $26 million in damage, and the May 21, 2001, destruction by arson of the University of Washington's Center for Urban Horticulture, that resulted in an estimated $3 million in damage. Other targets included U.S. Forest Service ranger stations, BLM wild-horse facilities, meat-processing companies, lumber companies, and a high-tension power line. Members of the group allegedly committed the attacks using improvised incendiary devices made from milk jugs, petroleum products, and homemade timers. Federal, state, and local law enforcement agencies participating in these investigations include the FBI, Bureau of Alcohol, Tobacco, Firearms, and Explosives, U.S. Forest Service, Bureau of Land Management, Oregon State Police, Eugene Police Department, and Portland Police Bureau. Additional arrests are expected in the ongoing investigation.

CONCLUSION

The preceding summary of terrorism-related events and investigations offers a picture of the FBI's response to domestic and international terrorism from 2002 through 2005. In keeping with a longstanding trend, domestic extremists carried out the majority of terrorist incidents during this period. Twenty three of the 24 recorded terrorist incidents were perpetrated by domestic terrorists. With the exception of white supremacist Sean Michael Gillespie's firebombing of a synagogue in Oklahoma City, Oklahoma, all of the domestic terrorist incidents were committed by special interest extremists active in the animal rights and environmental movements. The acts committed by these extremists typically targeted materials and facilities rather than persons. The sole international terrorist incident in the United States recorded for this period involved the attack by Hesham Hedayet, who fatally shot two people at the El Al ticket counter at Los Angeles International Airport.

The terrorist preventions for 2002 through 2005 paint a more diverse threat picture. Eight of the 14 recorded terrorist preventions stemmed from right-wing extremism, and included disruptions to plotting by individuals involved with the militia, white supremacist, constitutionalist and tax protestor, and anti-abortion movements. The remaining preventions included disruptions to plotting by an anarchist in Bellingham, Washington, who sought to bomb a U.S. Coast Guard station; a plot to attack an Islamic center in Pinellis Park, Florida; and a plot by prison-originated, Muslim convert group to attack U.S. military, Jewish, and Israeli targets in the greater Los Angeles area. In addition, three preventions involved individuals who sought to provide material support to foreign terrorist organizations, including al-Qa'ida, for attacks within the United States.

Whereas the violent, global jihadist movement manifested itself primarily in terrorist preventions in the United States from 2002 through 2005, internationally the movement claimed major attacks against U.S. and Western targets that resulted in American casualties. Most of these incidents were perpetrated by regional jihadist groups operating in primarily Muslim countries, including attacks perpetrated by Indonesia-based Jemaah Islamiya and al-Qa'ida in the Arabian Peninsula. The coordinated suicide bombing of London's mass transit system by homegrown jihadists, however, brought the violent jihadist movement and the tactic of suicide bombing to the heart of a major European capital.

In addition to these incidents and preventions, the years 2002 through 2005 saw the resolutions to high-profile prosecutions in the fight against terrorism. These included the December 2003 sentencing of the Lackawanna Six terror cell members, who received prison terms ranging from 7 to 10 years for providing material support or resources to al-Qa'ida; the October 4, 2002, sentencing of John Walker Lindh to 20 years in prison for conspiring with the Taliban to kill U.S. citizens; the January 30, 2003, sentencing of Richard Colvin Reid to life in prison for attempting to bomb a transcontinental flight using a shoe bomb; the sentencings in 2003 and 2004 of members of a Portland terrorist cell, who received prison terms ranging from 3 to 18 years for plotting to provide assistance to the Taliban and al-Qa'ida in fighting against U.S. troops in Afghanistan; the September 29, 2004, sentencing in Yemeni court of six individuals for their roles in the bombing of the USS Cole bombing, two of whom received the death penalty; the April 6, 2005, sentencing of Matthew Hale, leader of the white supremacist Creativity Movement, to 40 years in prison for solicitation of violence and obstruction of justice; the April 22, 2005, guilty plea of Zacaraias Moussaoui to his role in the 9/11 attack; the July 18, 2005, sentencing of Eric Robert Rudolph to life in prison for perpetrating several bombings, including the Centennial Olympic Park bombing in Atlanta, Georgia; the April 26, 2005, sentencing of Ali Al-Timimi to life in prison for encouraging others to receive military training from the designated foreign terrorist organization Lashkar-e-Tayyiba, to fight U.S. troops in Afghanistan; and the August 30, 2005, sentencing of white supremacist Sean Michael Gillespie to 39 years for firebombing a synagogue in Oklahoma City, Oklahoma.

FBI counterterrorism initiatives since the 9/11 terrorist attack have focused on preventing future attacks through the timely gathering, analysis, and dissemination of information; the facilitation of appropriate sharing of terrorism-related information between federal, state, and local partners; and the advancement of intelligence and law enforcement partnerships worldwide. FBI and U.S. counterterrorism organizational changes from 2002 through 2005 include the creation of the National Joint Terrorism Task Force; the establishment of the Foreign Terrorist Tracking Task Force; the establishment of the U.S. Department of Homeland Security through the signing of the Homeland Security Act; and the consolidation of government terrorist watch lists into the Terrorist Screening Center. In direct response to recommendations made by the 9/11 Commission, the Intelligence Reform and Terrorism Prevention Act of 2004 created the Office of the Director of National Intelligence, established the Director of National Intelligence as the head of the U.S. Intelligence Community, and instituted the National Counterterrorism Center as the primary federal entity for analyzing intelligence pertaining to transnational terrorism. These and other FBI and government initiatives are discussed in greater detail in the following In Focus retrospective of the FBI's counterterrorism program.

Casualties
of TERRORISM
1980-2005

WOUNDED	**14,038***
KILLED	**3,178**
TOTAL	**17,216***

12,017*

2977

1042

754

168

112

1980	1981	1982	1983	1984	1985	1986	1987	1988	1989	1990	1991	1992	1993	1994	1995	1996	1997	1998	1999	2000	2001	2002	2003	2004	2005
19 1	4 1	26 7	4 6	0 0	10 2	19 1	0 0	0 0	0 0	0 0	0 0	0 0	6 3	1	168	112	2	13 0	2 1	13 3	0 0	0 2	0 0	0 0	0 0

* The FBI uses 12,017 as an estimate for the number of those injured as a result of the September 11 attack; the exact number is unknown. Seventeen persons were infected by and recovered from exposure to the anthrax mailings during September-November 2001.

IN FOCUS

HISTORICAL OVERVIEW OF THE FBI'S COUNTERTERRORISM PROGRAM

INTRODUCTION

From its inception the FBI's counterterrorism program has had a mission to prevent planned acts of terrorism and, should a terrorist act occur, to mount a swift investigative response. During the first 75 years after the Bureau's founding in 1908, the terrorist threat to the United States came primarily from domestic sources. In recent decades, however, the problem of terrorism has developed into an international and global concern, and the FBI's counterterrorism program has evolved significantly as its counterterrorism responsibilities have increased. As a result, the FBI has steadily improved its ability to assess and counter the dynamic variety of domestic and international terrorist threats. The following summary provides a brief discussion of the definition of terrorism, followed by an historical overview of the FBI's counterterrorism efforts—from discrete, ad hoc responses to terrorist threats to its current top priority status—through a retrospective of the formative events and legislative initiatives that have contributed to its development.

TERRORISM: DEFINITIONS

Terrorism is not always self-evident. On July 4, 2002, Egyptian national Hesham Mohamed Hadayet shot and killed two people and wounded a third person at Los Angeles International Airport's El Al ticket counter before he was himself fatally shot by an airline security guard. Nine months later, on April 12, 2003, the U.S. Department of Justice publicly declared the shootings by Hadayet an act of terrorism. The FBI's investigation into the incident led to the conclusion that Hadayet, while unconnected to a formal terrorist organization, had committed an act of terrorism based upon his intention to advance the Palestinian cause in the Israel-Palestine conflict through the killing of civilians and the targeting of an airline owned by the Government of Israel. This case shows that investigation of an incident is sometimes necessary to determine motives or objectives behind a crime that would lead to its consideration as an act of terrorism. Beyond any consolation that understanding the nature of a crime can bring to survivors, to declare an incident a terrorist act is also to invoke a set of laws and punishments under which the incident may then be prosecuted.

Over the past several decades, the United States has begun to articulate terrorism as a distinctive category of criminal activity. The United States Code (USC) uses several definitions of terrorism that address specific legal situations, all of which have entered into the legal lexicon only since the 1970s. The FBI subdivides the terrorist threat facing the United States into the broad categories of international and domestic terrorism, each of which involves violent acts intended to intimidate or coerce a civilian population, or influence the policy or conduct of a government by mass destruction, assassination, or kidnapping. In cases of international terrorism, these acts transcend national boundaries in terms of the means by which they are accomplished, the persons they intend to intimidate, or the locale in which perpetrators operate (18 USC § 2331(1)). In cases of domestic terrorism, the FBI defines the source of coercion as a group or individual based and operating entirely within the United States, or its territories, without foreign direction (18 USC § 2331(5)). These legal definitions revolve around terrorism as coercion—as a violent means to a political end.

Another incident unrelated to terrorism provides comparative insight into the nature of terrorism. On the morning of February 21, 2003, an oil tanker exploded while unloading at a Staten Island oil depot. The blast killed two mariners and critically injured a third. News of the explosion sent prices on the New York Stock Exchange sharply lower on the assumption that a major terrorist incident had occurred. When details emerged in subsequent hours that revealed the explosion to have occurred accidentally, however, the stock market quickly recovered. The public anxiety and relief exhibited in the drop and recovery of trading on the stock exchange highlight two features of terrorism not otherwise covered by the legal definitions, and which to some extent reveal terrorism to be more about the intention than the violence behind the act. What the accident shared with terrorist acts was its dramatic impact. By virtue of its accidental nature, however, the explosion lacked the premeditated intent to do harm that marks terrorist attacks. The publicity and motivation associated with terrorism contribute to the anxiety a population can experience from an attack and also help to identify terrorism as an act of propaganda by which extremists bring notoriety to their causes.

In his September 20, 2001, Address to a Joint Session of Congress and the American People, President Bush assured his audience that in the present conflict with terrorism, violence would be met with "patient justice." The struggle against terrorism—especially that currently waged against al-Qa'ida—is one of endurance, and it is one in which the FBI is prepared to engage with unflagging persistence. Although the preeminent mission of protecting the United States from terrorist attack is changing the character of the FBI as a whole, an abiding strength of the FBI remains its tradition of excellence in vigorously investigating and prosecuting criminal acts. These traditional pursuits are essential to the disruption of terrorist activities, the dismantling of terrorist organizations, and, consequently, the prevention of future terrorist attacks. By combining a willingness to innovate with its traditional law enforcement responsibilities, the FBI continues to evolve in order to counter the varied forms of terrorism that threaten the interests and security of the United States.

35 YEARS OF TERRORISM

MARCH 1, 1971	FEBRUARY 5, 1974	AUGUST 5, 1974
BOMBING OF U.S. SENATE BUILDINGS	KIDNAPPING of PATTY HEARST by SYMBIONESE LIBERATION ARMY	ANTI-HIJACKING ACT PASSED
no injuries		

COUNTERING DOMESTIC TERROR
(1908-1982)

TERRORISM TRENDS

There are five traditional means by which the U.S. government fights terrorism: diplomacy, economic sanctions, military options, covert intelligence operations, and law enforcement action. The last two of these engage the resources of the FBI. Throughout its history, the FBI has directed the emphasis of its resources toward the most pressing national security and criminal activities affecting the country. Founded in 1908, the Bureau inherited subversive domestic political threats, including anarchism and communism, as concerns. Following the U.S. entry into World War I, the Bureau became the principle counterintelligence agency in the United States and, following the war, the investigation of a series of domestic terrorist bombings were the focus of its activities. These activities were eventually eclipsed by the property and violent crimes of the 1920s and early 1930s gangster era. World War II and the subsequent Cold War greatly increased the FBI's role in international affairs and counterintelligence. The Civil Rights Movement and the Vietnam War of the 1960s and early 1970s provoked criminal responses both from reactionary groups, such as the Ku Klux Klan, and antiwar extremists, such as the Weather Underground, respectively. Following strong criticism of FBI domestic security efforts by Congress in the mid-1970s, the Bureau's focus on domestic subversion gave way to new emphasis on organized crime and other criminal matters in the late 1970s and early 1980s.

Prior to the early 1980s, the FBI's terrorism-related investigations were dominated by domestic concerns. During the period from 1908 to 1982, the FBI dealt with two broad categories of domestic terrorism: right- and left-wing extremist groups. In the period between World War I and World War II, the domestic threat primarily came from right-wing groups, like the Ku Klux Klan, which often adhered to principles of racial supremacy or embraced antigovernment and antiregulatory beliefs in favor of individual freedoms. The FBI had little jurisdiction over these groups. In one case, the Bureau successfully developed a case against a ranking Klan official based on his violation of a law against interstate prostitution; there were no significant federal laws that forbade the Klan's terrorist activities at that time. The passage of significant civil rights legislation in the 1960s enabled the FBI to more effectively target the Klan and support successful prosecutions of Klan members for terrorist crimes.

JANUARY 24, 1975	JANUARY 29, 1975	MAY 1980
BOMBING of FRAUNCES TAVERN on WALL STREET	BOMBING of U.S. STATE DEPARTMENT BUILDING in WASHINGTON, D.C.	FIRST FBI JOINT TERRORISM TASK FORCE ESTABLISHED in NEW YORK
4 killed 53 injured	no injuries	

Beginning in the 1950s, the most serious domestic terrorist threat shifted to leftist-oriented extremist groups that generally professed a revolutionary socialist doctrine and viewed themselves as protectors of the people against the adverse effects of capitalism and U.S. foreign policies. Some of the more sensational terrorist events during this latter period included the November 1, 1950, attempted assassination of President Truman at Blair House by two members of the National Party of Puerto Rico. On March 1, 1954, members of the same group opened fire on a session of the U.S. House of Representatives, injuring five congressmen. The 1958 commandeering of a Cuban airliner in flight from Miami inaugurated a decade of hijackings by Cuban revolutionaries.

During the 1970s and 1980s, Croatian nationalists and the anti-Castro Cuban group Omega 7 arose as prominent terrorist threats. Leftist groups, however, continued to remain active during these decades and committed numerous bombings, including the prominent March 1, 1971, bombing of the U.S. Senate building and the January 29, 1975, bombing of the U.S. State Department building, both attributed to the Weather Underground, and the January 24, 1975, bombing of Fraunces Tavern on Wall Street by the Armed Forces for Puerto Rican National Liberation (FALN) that resulted in four deaths and 53 people injured. The threat from leftist groups receded by the late 1980s as law enforcement dismantled their infrastructures. The dissolution of the communist Soviet Union in December 1991 into the democratic Russian Federation with a free market economy further deprived many of these groups of their ideological foundation and patronage.

LEGISLATIVE ACTION

In this earliest period of FBI counterterrorism responses, there were few strong legislative tools available to handle the terrorist threats facing the United States. The 1917 Espionage Act and 1918 Sabotage Act addressed domestic subversion during wartime, but had no significant peacetime extension. Alien anarchists were apprehended and removed under various immigration statutes. National Security Action Memorandum 177, signed by President Kennedy on August 7, 1962, enhanced the U.S. government's foreign police training program, which has come to include counterterrorism measures. The Organized Crime Control Act of 1970 bears upon terrorism issues as they relate to the importation, manufacture, distribution, and storage of explosive materials (18 USC §§ 842-844). The Antihijacking Act of 1974 is noteworthy because it was the first law to specifically address an issue intimately connected to terrorism. And on April 10, 1982, President Reagan signed National Security Directive 30 (NSD 30), which gave lead agency counterterrorism responsibilities and crisis management in terrorist attacks to the FBI under the U.S. Department of Justice.

JANUARY 1982	APRIL 10, 1982	FEBRUARY 13, 1983
FBI HOSTAGE RESCUE TEAM ESTABLISHED	NATIONAL SECURITY DECISION DIRECTIVE 30 gives lead agency counterterrorism responsibilities to the FBI (U.S. DEPARTMENT of JUSTICE)	FIRST RECORDED ATTACK of RIGHT-WING ANTIGOVERNMENT GROUP (Sheriff's Posse Comitatus in Medina, North Dakota)

FBI INITIATIVES

In the decades leading up to the 1980s, the FBI had not yet begun to structure its resources in terrorism-specific terms. Following two significant anarchist bombing attacks in the spring of 1919, the U.S. Department of Justice established a General Intelligence Division, headed by J. Edgar Hoover, to gather and analyze intelligence concerning communist, anarchist, and other radical threats in the United States. In 1920, the General Intelligence Division was incorporated into what was then known as the Bureau of Investigation. Hoover continued to head the division and was appointed the Bureau's Assistant Director under Director William Burns (1922-24), a position he held until his own appointment as Director, a position he held from 1924 to 1972. Discontinued at that time, the division was re-established in 1935 to monitor communist and fascist activities.

The General Intelligence Division went through several name changes during the 1940s and 1950s—the National Defense Division in 1940, the Security Division in 1942, and the Domestic Security Division in 1951—that tended to reflect the FBI's responsibilities for domestic security. Until 1973, this division oversaw the FBI's responsibilities for domestic security, counterintelligence, and counterterrorism. In 1973, in response to criticism of FBI programs to disrupt radical groups, the Domestic Security Division was split into a General Investigative Division and an Intelligence Division. In 1977 the newly created Criminal Investigative Division assumed domestic terrorism responsibilities on the principle that investigations into domestic radical groups were predicated upon criminal activity. In 1982, in response to NSD 30, Director William H. Webster (1978-87) named counterterrorism an FBI priority program.[1] The responsibilities for counterterrorism continued to reside in the Criminal Investigative Division, which developed a Terrorism Section comprised of a domestic unit and several international counterterrorism units.

Like the early acts of legislation that have since served as the foundation for terrorism-related amendments, the FBI initiated several programs over this period that have come to play significant roles in its evolving counterterrorism efforts. One innovation during this early period was the deployment of forensic specialists to the site of an investigation. The first incarnation of this rapid deployment capability was the Disaster Squad established on June 24, 1940, to assist civilian authorities in identifying persons killed in a Virginia plane crash. Since then, these deployment capabilities have expanded to other areas of FBI operations including the Hostage Rescue Team, the Rapid Deployment Teams, and the Fly Team, which support counterterrorism operations, as well as the Laboratory Division's Evidence Response Teams and Hazardous Materials Response Teams, which support forensic investigations.

[1] The designation of "Priority Programs" began under the management reform initiated by Director Clarence M. Kelley (1973-78) to focus FBI resources on the most pressing matters. At the time, these included white collar crime, organized crime, and foreign counterintelligence. Counterterrorism became a Priority Program in 1982.

APRIL 18, 1983	SEPTEMBER 16, 1983	OCTOBER 23, 1983
BOMBING of the U.S. EMBASSY in BEIRUT, LEBANON	WELLS-FARGO ARMORED CAR ROBBERY NETS LOS MACHETEROS $7.2 MILLION	BOMBING of the MARINE BARRACKS in BEIRUT, LEBANON
63 killed		241 U.S. Marines killed

In the middle of the 20th century, the FBI also laid the foundations for coordinating investigations and sharing information with international law enforcement and intelligence partners when it established its Legal Attaché, or "Legat" program. The origins of the Legat program lie in the FBI's early intelligence responsibilities. On June 24, 1940, prior to the United States' involvement in World War II, President Roosevelt issued a directive for the FBI to assume responsibility for countering Axis movements in the Western Hemisphere and gathering intelligence about other developments in that sphere of responsibility. In response, Director Hoover created the Special Intelligence Service (SIS) within the FBI. The effort was successful both in gathering intelligence and countering Axis intelligence activities. In 1946, President Truman terminated the SIS and reassigned its duties to the newly created Central Intelligence Group, later renamed the Central Intelligence Agency, as part of his centralization of foreign intelligence collection. The FBI, however, was allowed to maintain a number of its liaison offices in order to communicate with foreign police and intelligence services. By January 1953, FBI Legats operated in U.S. embassies in London, Paris, Madrid, Havana, Mexico City, and Rio de Janeiro. The number of Legat offices has continued to grow in recognition of their valued assistance in tracking terrorist threats and bringing investigative resources swiftly to bear on terrorist and other incidents overseas.

Cooperation among law enforcement and intelligence agencies is now widely recognized as essential to a comprehensive plan to prevent and respond to terrorism. Internationally, in order to create a corps of advocates for best law enforcement practices worldwide, in 1935 the Bureau began training law enforcement officers from foreign countries at its National Academy in Quantico, Virginia. Domestically, the FBI operationally cooperates with other law enforcement agencies in part through Joint Terrorism Task Forces (JTTFs), whose strength lies in combining the national and international investigative resources of the FBI with the street-level expertise of state and local law enforcement agencies. The first JTTF was formed in New York City in 1980 in response to domestic terrorism threats posed by such organizations as the Puerto Rican separatist group FALN and the anti-Castro Cuban group Omega 7.

MAY 1984	SEPTEMBER 20, 1984	DECEMBER 8, 1984
COMPREHENSIVE CRIME CONTROL ACT GIVES FBI JURISDICTION to PURSUE TERRORISTS WHO TAKE AMERICANS HOSTAGE	BOMBING of the U.S. EMBASSY ANNEX in BEIRUT, LEBANON 14 killed	"THE ORDER" LEADER ROBERT JAY MATHEWS DIES in CONFRONTATION with LAW ENFORCEMENT

THE EMERGENCE OF INTERNATIONAL TERRORISM (1983-1992)

TERRORISM TRENDS

For the decade from 1983-1992, major acts of terrorism against U.S. interests took place overseas. The FBI recognized state-sponsored and autonomous terrorist organizations as the two significant sources of international terrorism. Both types of organizations remain threats today.

State-sponsored terrorism refers to those countries that violate international law by using terrorism as a tool of foreign policy.[2]   One of the most infamous acts of state-sponsored terrorism during this period occurred on December 21, 1988, with the bombing of Pan Am flight 103 in mid-air over Lockerbie, Scotland. The bombing killed all 259 people aboard the Boeing 747 aircraft and 11 people on the ground. In November 1991, following an extensive investigation by the FBI and other U.S. and foreign police authorities, a U.S. grand jury indicted two Libyan intelligence officers for the crime. The two were tried in the Netherlands under Scottish law. On January 31, 2001, the court acquitted one of the officers due to insufficient evidence, but convicted the other officer, Abdel Basset Ali al-Megrahi, of murder and issued him a mandatory life sentence. In August 2003 the Government of Libya agreed to pay $2.7 billion in restitution to the families of the victims.

Foreign terrorist organizations (FTOs) are autonomous, generally transnational groups that maintain their own personnel, infrastructures, financial arrangements, and training facilities. FTOs are often formed to pursue nationalistic agendas that can span the political spectrum, and their operational capabilities range from organizations with extremely limited resources and memberships of fewer than 100, to others with thousands of supporters and substantial sources of aid. FTOs committed two major bombings in 1983 and a series of prominent hijackings in the decade that followed, drawing legislative and law enforcement attention to international terrorism. On April 18, 1983, members of Lebanese Hizballah bombed the U.S. Embassy in Beirut, Lebanon. The attack resulted in 63 deaths, including those of 17 U.S. citizens. Six months later, on October 23, Hizballah bombed the U.S. Marine barracks in Beirut. The blast killed 301, of whom 241 were U.S. Marines. Hijackings during the 1980s, most notably committed by Hizballah[3] and the Abu Nidal Organization in the Middle East and South Asia, targeted U.S. airliners, or American citizens on foreign carriers, and frequently resulted in extended hostage situations and civilian fatalities.

Although international terrorism against U.S. interests took place overseas during this period, the FBI began investigations into the use of the United States as a staging area

[2] At the end of 2005, the U.S. Department of State designated six nations–Cuba, Iran, Libya, North Korea, Sudan, and Syria– as state sponsors of terrorism. The U.S. Department of State formally removed Iraq from the list of state sponsors of terrorism on October 20, 2004.

[3] Since its founding in 1982, Hizballah's numerous anti-U.S. attacks overseas made it responsible for the deaths of more Americans than any other terrorist group in the world prior to September 11, 2001.

SEPTEMBER 14, 1985	AUGUST 27, 1986	APRIL 16, 1987
TWA 847 HIJACKED U.S. Navy Diver killed	OMNIBUS DIPLOMATIC SECURITY and ANTITERRORISM ACT EXPANDS FBI JURISDICTION to INCLUDE VIOLENCE against U.S. NATIONALS ABROAD	FIRST FBI RECORDED ALF ATTACK in the UNITED STATES (Davis, California)

or source of arms for terrorist operations and activities overseas. An example of this is the 1990 conviction in Boston court of two U.S. citizens and a citizen of the Republic of Ireland of conspiracy to violate the Arms Export Control Act and of conspiracy to injure and destroy foreign property. Until their arrest in 1989, these individuals had engaged in the research and development of an anti-helicopter missile system for use by the Provisional Irish Republican Army in its attacks against British targets in Northern Ireland and elsewhere.

LEGISLATIVE ACTION

In the mid-1980s Congress passed several legislative initiatives that expanded the FBI's jurisdiction to include U.S. interests overseas. The Comprehensive Crime Control Act of 1984 gave the FBI jurisdiction to pursue terrorists who have taken Americans hostage, regardless of where the incident occurred. Also in 1984, the Act to Combat International Terrorism established the Rewards for Justice Program, authorizing the Secretary of State to issue rewards of up to $5 million for information that prevents or favorably resolves acts of international terrorism against U.S. persons or property worldwide. The Omnibus Diplomatic Security and Antiterrorism Act of August 27, 1986, expanded the FBI's jurisdiction to include homicide or violence against U.S. citizens abroad. The Biological Weapons Anti-Terrorism Act of 1989 granted federal jurisdiction with respect to developing, transferring, and possessing biological weapons.

FBI INITIATIVES

The FBI's international responsibilities had been increasing in the decades leading up to the 1980s as drug trafficking, organized crime, and terrorism investigations frequently crossed national boundaries. With respect to international liaison activities, in 1983 Congress authorized the U.S. Department of State's Antiterrorism Assistance Program as part of a major initiative against international terrorism. As part of this program the FBI began to provide counterterrorism training to law enforcement and security personnel of selected friendly foreign governments at the FBI Academy at Quantico. This training served both to strengthen bilateral ties and to increase respect for human rights by sharing with civilian authorities modern, humane, and effective counterterrorism techniques.

Another significant development within the Bureau resulted from an incident during the 1972 Summer Olympic Games held in Munich, Germany, in which Palestinian gunmen

JUNE 1987	DECEMBER 21, 1988	OCTOBER 13, 1989
FAWAZ YOUNIS RENDERED from CYPRUS for HIJACKING a ROYAL JORDANIAN AIRLINER	BOMBING of PAN AM 103 over LOCKERBIE, SCOTLAND 217 Americans killed	TERRORIST THREAT WARNING SYSTEM (TTWS) ESTABLISHED

associated with the terrorist group Black September took 11 Israeli athletes hostage in the Olympic Village. The gunmen killed their captives in the rescue attempt that followed. This incident led the FBI to anticipate the possibility of a similar international act of terrorism during the 1984 Summer Olympics to be held in Los Angeles. In 1983 the FBI began training its Hostage Rescue Team (HRT), which was in operation by the start of the games. Based at the FBI Academy at Quantico, the HRT has the mission of responding within four hours of notification by the Director or his designate to any extraordinary hostage crisis occurring within the United States. Since its inception, the HRT has been deployed in support of FBI terrorism, violent criminal, foreign counterintelligence, and other investigations.

Recognizing the importance of warning as a component in the FBI's efforts to prevent acts of terrorism, on October 13, 1989, the FBI established the Terrorist Threat Warning System (TTWS) for the dissemination of terrorist threat information to the U.S. Intelligence Community[4] and state and local law enforcement agencies.[5]

THE GLOBALIZATION OF TERRORISM (1993-2001)

TERRORISM TRENDS

Until the 1990s, terrorist targets had historically been selected for reasons of their vulnerability and symbolism. Indiscrimination generally remained an unintended consequence of terrorist attacks. During the 1990s, however, the nature of domestic and international terrorism underwent recognizable changes in tactics and methodologies as terrorists aimed to inflict massive and indiscriminate casualties upon civilian populations. The terrorist trend toward higher levels of casualties came at a time when interest was growing among domestic and international extremists in weapons of mass destruction (WMD). The movement toward acquiring and using WMD became a reality on March 20, 1995, when the Japanese group Aum Shinrikyo launched a series of sarin nerve gas attacks in Tokyo's subway system. The incidents resulted in 12 deaths and approximately 5,000 exposures. The FBI provided investigative assistance to Japanese law enforcement and intelligence agencies in response to the incident. These attacks suggested the wide range of weapons available to contemporary terrorists and raised the specter of a similar attack in the United States.

Another trend during this period altered the paradigm that only international terrorists operating outside of the United States committed major acts of terrorism. With respect to domestic terrorism, left-wing political groups and *special interest terrorism*—that is, terrorism committed by extremists who use violence to compel society to change its attitudes

[4] The "U.S. Intelligence Community" refers to those Executive Branch organizations engaged in U.S. national intelligence efforts. The Community includes the Central Intelligence Agency, National Security Agency, Defense Intelligence Agency, intelligence elements of the departments of Defense, State, Treasury, Energy, Homeland Security, and the FBI (CIA, *Factbook on Intelligence*, 2006).

[5] On January 4, 1999, the FBI integrated the TTWS into the National Threat Warning System (NTWS).

NOVEMBER 5, 1990	FEBRUARY 26, 1993	JUNE 24, 1993
ASSASSINATION of RABBI MEIR KAHANE, FOUNDER of the JEWISH DEFENSE LEAGUE, in NEW YORK CITY	BOMBING of the WORLD TRADE CENTER in NEW YORK CITY 6 killed 1,000+ injured	ARREST of EIGHT SUBJECTS PLOTTING to BOMB NEW YORK LANDMARKS

about specific causes—asserted themselves during the 1990s. Anarchists reemerged in the United States during this period and caused much of the criminal disruption during the 1999 World Trade Organization meeting in Seattle. The majority of domestic terrorism incidents from 1993 to 2001 were attributable to the left-wing special interest movements the Animal Liberation Front (ALF) and the Earth Liberation Front (ELF). Right-wing extremism, however, primarily in the form of domestic militias and conservative special interest causes, began to overtake left-wing extremism as the most dangerous, if not the most prolific, domestic terrorist threat to the country during the 1990s. In contrast to the ALF and the ELF, which have pursued a philosophy that avoids physical violence in favor of acts of property damage that cause their victims economic harm, right-wing extremists pursued a qualitatively different method of operation by targeting people.

The April 19, 1995, bombing of the Alfred P. Murrah Federal Building in Oklahoma City, Oklahoma, brought the threat of right-wing terrorism to the forefront of American law enforcement attention. The Oklahoma City bombing, which killed 168 people and injured 642 others, was an extreme manifestation of a grass-roots antigovernment movement that became prominent during the 1990s. Several factors fueled the growth of this movement, including the passage of gun control legislation, fears of increased United Nations involvement in domestic affairs, and several confrontations between members of right-wing groups and law enforcement officers at Waco, Texas, and Ruby Ridge, Idaho. These confrontations inspired Timothy McVeigh and Terry Nichols to carry out the Oklahoma City bombing, which coincided with the second anniversary of the destruction of the Branch Davidian compound near Waco. The FBI aggressively pursued the prosecutions of McVeigh and Nichols, and the two were eventually convicted for their roles in the bombing. McVeigh was executed on June 11, 2001, marking the first federal execution in 38 years.

The motivations behind another series of bombings in the mid-1990s illustrate the increasing prominence of terrorism in support of conservative special interest causes during this decade. On July 27, 1996, an explosion in Olympic Centennial Park killed two and injured 112 during the closing days of the Summer Olympics held in Atlanta, Georgia. Early the next year, two more bombings occurred: the first, on January 16, 1997, at a Birmingham, Alabama, health clinic; the second, on February 21, 1997, at the Otherside Lounge, a nightclub patronized by Atlanta's gay community. These latter bombings were distinctive in that the terrorist used secondary explosive devices with an apparent intent to target emergency responders. On May 31, 2003, Top Ten Fugitive Eric Robert Rudolph was arrested in North Carolina on suspicion of having committed the bombings; Rudolph pled guilty to these attacks and received a life sentence for his crimes.

The bombings in Oklahoma City, Atlanta, and Birmingham also brought an awareness of a new type of threat from those who may be sympathetic to extreme political or social ideologies, but who commit acts of violence outside of the auspices of structured terrorist organizations or without the prior approval or knowledge of these groups' leaders. The roles of McVeigh and Nichols in the Oklahoma City bombing, and the bombings by

APRIL 19, 1995	JUNE 21, 1995	APRIL 24, 1996
BOMBING of the OKLAHOMA CITY FEDERAL BUILDING 168 killed 642 injured	PRESIDENTIAL DECISION DIRECTIVE 39 CONFIRMED and CLARIFIED FBI'S COUNTERTERRORISM ROLE	ANTI-TERRORISM and EFFECTIVE DEATH PENALTY ACT PASSED

Rudolph, exemplify the FBI's "lone offender" category of terrorist for those who engage in terrorist activities free from organizational guidance.

With respect to international terrorism, terrorist organizations, sometimes with state sponsorship, continued to attack U.S. military targets overseas. A November 13, 1995, truck bomb killed seven people, including five Americans, and injured at least 34 U.S. citizens at the Office of the Program Manager/Saudi Arabian National Guard building in Riyadh, Saudi Arabia. Seven months later, on June 25, 1996, members of Saudi Hizballah bombed the Khobar Towers in Dhahran, Saudi Arabia, where Western military personnel resided. The explosion killed 19 U.S. service personnel and injured over 350 others. These bombings highlighted force protection issues, to which the U.S. government responded by "hardening" its official establishments overseas.

During the 1990s, the U.S. Intelligence Community began to recognize a trend in international terrorism away from state sponsors of terrorism and FTOs to those of loosely affiliated extremists, whose ad hoc, autonomous nature tended to shield them from infiltration and disruption. This new aspect of international terrorism first presented itself in the February 26, 1993, bombing of New York City's World Trade Center. The blast killed six people, injured more than 1,000, and caused millions of dollars in damage. In a subsequent plot based out of the Philippines, the New York bombing's operational mastermind, Ramzi Ahmed Yousef, along with two co-conspirators, planned to destroy simultaneously as many as 12 American jumbo jets in flight over the Pacific. Yousef conducted a trial run of the "Manila Air" plot on December 11, 1994, when a test explosive killed a Japanese businessman on board a Philippine airliner in flight to Tokyo. A few months later, on February 7, 1995, Yousef was apprehended in Islamabad, Pakistan, by Pakistani officials who were working with FBI assistance and rendered back to the United States. In January 1998, Yousef was sentenced to 240 years plus a life sentence in prison for his roles in the 1993 World Trade Center bombing and the "Manila Air" plot.

By the late 1990s, the interwoven violence and self-perpetuating nature of terrorism, in which a terrorist act in one location can elicit a sympathetic response elsewhere, regardless of national boundaries, became apparent. An example of the web of terrorism can be seen in the events involving Shayk Omar Abdel Rahman, the spiritual leader of Egypt's Al-Gama'a al-Islamiyya (AGAI) militant group. Investigation into the World Trade Center bombing uncovered unrelated plotting by Shayk Rahman and his followers to bomb landmarks throughout New York City in the summer of 1993 and to assassinate Egyptian President Hosni Mubarak during a visit to New York in 1994. In January 1996 Shayk Rahman and nine co-conspirators were convicted of the plots, and Shayk Rahman himself received a life sentence plus 55 years. On November 17, 1997, six AGAI members killed 58 foreign tourists at the Temple of Hatshepsut near Luxor, Egypt. Although no Americans were among the victims, the attack was intended to apply pressure on the United States to release Shayk Rahman from incarceration. The web-like nature of ter-

APRIL 24, 1996	JULY 27, 1996	JULY 1996
FBI COUNTERTERRORISM CENTER ESTABLISHED at FBI HEADQUARTERS	BOMBING of CENTENNIAL OLYMPIC PARK 2 killed 112 injured	FBI COMPUTER INVESTIGATION and INFRASTRUCTURE THREAT CENTER (CITAC) ESTABLISHED at FBI HEADQUARTERS

rorism underscores the need for vigilance and international cooperation in countering terrorist groups. While the serial plotting of Shayk Rahman highlights the importance of relentlessly pursuing the arrest and prosecution of individual terrorists in order to prevent them from perpetrating future acts, the related attack near Luxor underscores the importance of a cooperative international effort to control terrorism.

As a result of the plots by Ramzi Yousef and Shayk Rahman, the FBI began to focus investigative attention on the then-emerging phenomenon of Sunni extremism and its operational manifestation in loosely affiliated groups devoted to violent international jihad. The international jihad movement, which interprets jihad ("struggle") in militant terms, is composed of individuals of varying nationalities, ethnicities, and terrorist group affiliations. These individuals find common purpose in seeking to establish states ruled by *sharia* (conservative Islamic) law and free of Western influence. As precedent, Afghanistan's resistance to the Soviet invasion of 1979 attracted foreign fighters, who viewed their participation in the regional conflict as a defense both of their Muslim brethren and of Islam. The Soviet Union's eventual withdrawal from Afghanistan in 1989 led to the establishment of Afghanistan's Taliban regime and inspired former Arab-Afghan *mujahidin* ("holy warriors") to focus their zeal upon other international conflicts that involved Muslim populations. This globalization of violent jihad contributed to the globalization of terrorist groups, which recruited *mujahidin* to engage in militant struggle with operations that transcended national boundaries.

Influenced by radical leaders such as Usama Bin Ladin, former Arab-Afghan *mujahidin* integrated into the international terrorist infrastructure known as al-Qa'ida ("the Root"). In the early 1990s the al-Qa'ida network began issuing *fatwahs* (religious opinions based upon Islamic law) to its members and associates calling for the deposition of the Saudi monarchy and the forced removal of U.S. and other Western forces from the Arabian Peninsula. Bin Ladin first stated his declaration of war against the United States in a twelve-page *banyan* ("statement") issued on August 22, 1996, in which he offered a "final warning" for all American troops to leave the land of the "Two Holy Places" (Mecca and Medina in Saudi Arabia) or else face military action by the same people who drove the Soviets out of Afghanistan. Bin Ladin's rhetoric since then, including a 1998 statement urging Muslims to "kill the Americans and their allies–civilians and military," revealed a steady shift toward greater indiscrimination in al-Qa'ida's targeting.

With the exception of the 1995 Oklahoma City bombing, the major terrorist acts or attempts against U.S. interests leading into the 21st century stemmed from militant Islamic jihad, guided directly or indirectly by al-Qa'ida. These include the following:

- On August 7, 1998, al-Qa'ida operatives carried out near-simultaneous bombings of the U.S. embassies in Nairobi, Kenya, and Dar es Salaam, Tanzania. These attacks, which took place against targets considered "soft"

FEBRUARY 26, 1998	AUGUST 7, 1998	OCTOBER 16, 1998
FBI CITAC REPLACED by NATIONAL INFRASTRUCTURE PROTECTION CENTER	BOMBING of U.S. EMBASSIES in KENYA and TANZANIA 12 Americans killed 7 injured	NATIONAL DOMESTIC PREPAREDNESS OFFICE ESTABLISHED

and in low-threat countries, resulted in 224 deaths and 5,722 injuries. The small number of Americans among the casualties (12 dead and seven wounded) highlighted the indiscriminate nature of, and collateral damage inflicted by, large-scale terrorist attacks even when directed against specific targets.

- On December 14, 1999, U.S. border guards at Port Angeles, Washington, arrested Ahmed Ressam as he attempted to smuggle explosives into the United States from Canada. Investigation by the FBI and other domestic and foreign law enforcement agencies revealed that Ressam had attended al-Qa'ida training camps in Afghanistan and was part of an Algerian terrorist cell based in Canada that had plotted to detonate explosives at Los Angeles International Airport.

- On October 12, 2000, in the port of Aden, Yemen, pilots of a bomb-laden boat pulled alongside the *USS Cole* at midship and detonated their explosives in a suicide attack against the destroyer, killing 17 and injuring at least 40 crew members. Investigation revealed that the incident followed an unsuccessful attack on January 3, 2000, against the *USS The Sullivans*. The alleged conspirators in the *Sullivans* and *Cole* attacks were al-Qa'ida operatives who trained in its terrorist camps in Afghanistan during the 1990s. The *Cole* bombing highlighted al-Qa'ida's resolve and revealed the network's resourcefulness and ingenuity in developing asymmetrical tactics to strike a more powerful and technologically more advanced target.

LEGISLATIVE ACTION

Motivated by the World Trade Center and Oklahoma City bombings, the U.S. government took a number of executive and legislative steps that directed the focus of future law enforcement activity to include prevention before an incident, as well as the apprehension and conviction of those responsible after an incident has occurred.

On June 21, 1995, President Clinton issued Presidential Decision Directive 39 (PDD 39), which clarified the FBI's designation as the lead U.S. government agency for dealing with terrorism against Americans in the United States and overseas. On April 24, 1996, the U.S. government passed the Anti-Terrorism and Effective Death Penalty Act (AEDPA), which addressed domestic terrorism by increasing the protection afforded to federal workers and expanding criminal statutes relating to explosives. The AEDPA's most significant contributions, however, concerned the expansion of the FBI's investigative authority into international acts of terrorism and the activities of international terrorist groups as they occurred within the United States. These contributions included provisions addressing

JANUARY 4, 1999	NOVEMBER 21, 1999	DECEMBER 14, 1999
EXPANDED NATIONAL THREAT WARNING SYSTEM (NTWS) REPLACES TTWS	FBI COUNTERTERRORISM DIVISION ESTABLISHED at FBI HEADQUARTERS	ARREST OF AHMED RESSAM ENTERING the UNITED STATES from CANADA with EXPLOSIVES

the prevention of entry into and deportation of alien terrorists from the United States and the prosecution of those who provide material support to a designated terrorist organization.

In a reflection of the changing dynamics of terrorism, the U.S. government responded legislatively and administratively to the WMD threat. In 1996 the passage of the Defense Against Weapons of Mass Destruction Act—also known as the Nunn-Lugar-Domenici Program after the three senators who sponsored the legislation—established first-responder training. On May 28, 1998, President Clinton issued Presidential Decision Directives 62 and 63 (PDDs 62 and 63). PDD 62 established guidelines for FBI-led interagency cooperation in the detection, prevention, and consequence management of terrorist incidents involving WMD. PDD 63 set objectives for protecting the nation's infrastructure from attack. On October 16, 1998, Congress established the interagency National Domestic Preparedness Office at FBI Headquarters to coordinate federal assistance programs and to streamline the process of delivering that assistance to state and local communities in the event of a catastrophic terrorist attack.

FBI INITIATIVES

During the 1990s, the FBI's counterterrorism program underwent several organizational transformations that led to the eventual creation of a Counterterrorism Division within the Bureau. On March 18, 1994, the Intelligence Division was renamed the National Security Division, retaining foreign counterintelligence responsibilities and taking over the Criminal Investigative Division's domestic and international terrorism responsibilities. In 1998, the FBI established a strategic plan that set flexible investigative priorities within a three-tiered structure: Tier 1 for criminal and intelligence matters—including terrorism—that threatened national or economic security; Tier 2 for offenses that involved criminal enterprises, public corruption, and violations of civil rights; and Tier 3 for violations that affected individual property. The priority given to counterterrorism was reflected in FBI Director Louis J. Freeh's (1993-2001) October 29, 1999, transfer of the National Security Division's counterterrorism components into two new complementary divisions—the Counterterrorism Division and the Investigative Services Division—that took responsibility for most of the old division's operational and analytical functions, respectively.

The FBI's liaison activities also evolved during this period. Domestically, the New York JTTF took part in several high-profile terrorism-related investigations in the mid-1990s. Its proven value led to the expansion of the JTTF program to other field offices and spurred an increase in the participation of federal, state, and local member agencies in the task forces. In 1996, JTTFs received executive endorsement when President Clinton issued PDD 39 authorizing the Bureau to provide a coordinated law enforcement effort. PDDs 62 and 63 led to the establishment of the multi-agency Domestic Emergency Support Team (DEST), coordinated by the FBI and deployed by the FBI Director.[6] On

[6] The FBI also participates in the Foreign Emergency Support Team (FEST) coordinated by the U.S. Department of State.

OCTOBER 12, 2000	JUNE 11, 2001	SEPTEMBER 11, 2001
BOMBING of *USS COLE* 17 killed at least 40 injured	OKLAHOMA CITY BOMBER TIMOTHY MCVEIGH EXECUTED; FIRST FEDERAL EXECUTION in 38 YEARS	AL-QA'IDA OPERATIVES HIJACK and CRASH FOUR COMMERCIAL AIRLINERS into WORLD TRADE CENTER, PENTAGON, and STONYCREEK TOWNSHIP 2,972 killed

November 20, 1998, a technologically upgraded Strategic Information and Operations Center (SIOC) opened at FBI Headquarters to manage and monitor major events and crises, including those requiring a counterterrorism response.[7]

The bombings of the World Trade Center, the Khobar Towers, and the East African embassies made clear the importance of international cooperation in investigations of international acts of terrorism. As part of its cooperative efforts with international law enforcement, Director Freeh expanded the number of Legat offices to 42 by the spring of 2001. The FBI also took lead-agency responsibility for establishing the International Law Enforcement Academy (ILEA) to provide professional law enforcement education to foreign nationals overseas including counterterrorism components; the first ILEA opened in 1994 in Budapest, Hungary.

Until the last decade of the 20th century, criminal threats within the United States set a domestic agenda for the FBI. The East African embassy bombings, however, elevated al-Qa'ida to the highest priority of FBI counterterrorism. On November 4, 1998, Usama Bin Ladin was indicted for his role in the embassy bombings, and the U.S. Department of State issued an unprecedented $5 million reward for his apprehension.[8] In April 1999 the FBI placed Bin Ladin on its Ten Most Wanted Fugitives List, and in the same year established a dedicated Bin Ladin Unit at FBI Headquarters.

In 1998, the FBI formalized its ability to respond to international terrorist incidents by creating Rapid Deployment Teams (RDTs), which swiftly bring investigative personnel and resources to attack sites where an FBI presence is otherwise wanting or in need of augmentation. These teams are capable of organizing and establishing field command posts, forensically exploring crime scenes, and conducting criminal investigations. By March 28, 2001, the FBI had established five RDTs in four of its major field offices.

"Cyberterrorism," or the use of cyber tools to shut down critical national infrastructures for the purpose of coercing or intimidating a government or civilian population, emerged as a threat at the end of the last century. While terrorist groups have not yet employed cyber tools as a weapon against critical U.S. infrastructures, their acquisition of computer expertise and reliance on information technology to formulate plans, raise funds, spread propaganda, and engage in secure communications represent clear warning signs. In 1996 the FBI established the Computer Investigation and Infrastructure Threat Center (CIITC) at FBI Headquarters. On February 26, 1998, President Clinton expanded CIITC into the multi-agency National Infrastructure Protection Center (NIPC), to serve as the focal point for the government's effort to warn of and respond to domestic and international cyber intrusions.[9]

[7] SIOC was originally conceived in 1987 in response to prison riots at Oakdale, Louisiana, and Atlanta, Georgia. These concurrent incidents suggested the need to provide integrated support to FBI field offices in major crises. SIOC first became operational under the aegis of the Criminal Investigative Division on January 20, 1989, in time for the inauguration of the elder President Bush. In subsequent years, management of SIOC transferred to the Investigative Services Division and the Critical Incident Response Group before being integrated into the Counterterrorism Division in April 2003.

[8] Four al-Qa'ida members have received life sentences for conspiring to kill Americans in the East African embassy bombings. Two other suspects await trial, and 16 others, including Usama Bin Ladin, stand indicted.

[9] NIPC now operates under the aegis of the Department of Homeland Security. In December 2001, Director Robert S. Mueller III approved creation of the FBI's Cyber Division to address cyber investigations formerly addressed by the Counterterrorism and Criminal Investigative Divisions.

SEPTEMBER 23, 2001	FALL 2001	OCTOBER 7, 2001
EXECUTIVE ORDER 13224 ENACTED BLOCKING TERRORIST ASSESTS	ANTHRAX-TAINTED LETTERS SENT through U.S. POSTAL SYSTEM FIRST CRIMINAL USE of a BIOLOGICAL TOXIN 18 infected 5 deaths	UNITED STATES BEGINS MILITARY ACTION in AFGHANISTAN

THE "WAR ON TERRORISM" (SEPTEMBER 11, 2001-PRESENT)

TERRORISM TRENDS

Beginning in the late 1950s the most serious terrorist threat to U.S. civil aviation came in the form of hijackings of commercial aircraft. In these incidents, the aircraft provided hijackers both transportation to diverted destinations and a ready supply of hostages for leverage in their negotiations with government authorities. By the late 1980s—as seen in the 1988 bombing of Pan Am flight 103 over Lockerbie, Scotland, and in the prevented "Manila Air" plot of 1994—the threat to civil aviation began to include the targeting of commercial aircraft and their passengers and crews for destruction.

On the morning of September 11, 2001, al-Qa'ida directed its ruthless ingenuity toward the further exploitation of civil aviation when 19 of its operatives hijacked four U.S. commercial airliners for use as suicide weapons against selected political, military, and economic targets on the U.S. East Coast. The hijackers used knives, boxcutters, and possibly pepper spray to commandeer the aircraft. Three of the aircraft struck their targets, destroying the Twin Towers of the World Trade Center in New York City and badly damaging the Pentagon in Arlington, Virginia. The fourth aircraft crashed into a remote field in Stonycreek Township, Pennsylvania, as passengers attempted to regain control of the airplane. All of the passengers on each of the aircraft were killed in the attack, as were more than 2,500 people in the Twin Towers and the Pentagon. In total, 2,972 people died in the September 11 attack, making it the most deadly act of terrorism ever committed.[10] The September 11 attack also marked the first known suicide terrorist attack carried out in the United States since the FBI began keeping terrorist records.

The threat of terrorism is expected to continue from both international and domestic sources. Internationally, at least two operational trends are evident in the militant Islamic jihad movement. First is a preference for high-casualty, high-profile attacks directed against lower-risk, unofficial, so-called "soft" targets, as traditional military and diplomatic targets become increasingly hardened. Second, the dissolution of much of al-Qa'ida's structure by international military and law enforcement efforts has resulted in the dispersal of its multinational trainees to pursue their own regional agendas. The following terrorist incidents from September 11, 2001, through 2005 may involve both trends:

- On October 12, 2002, a nightclub bombing on the Indonesian island of Bali killed approximately 200 people, including seven Americans, and on August 5, 2003, a bombing of the JW Marriott Hotel in Jakarta, Indonesia, resulted in 15 deaths. Both of these bombings have been attributed to mem-

[10] This number does not include the 19 hijackers, all of whom died in the attack.

OCTOBER 10, 2001	OCTOBER 26, 2001	DECEMBER 12, 2001
FBI ESTABLISHES MOST WANTED TERRORIST LIST	USA PATRIOT ACT PASSED into LAW	ZACARIAS MOUSSAOUI INDICTED on SIX COUNTS of CONSPIRACY for HIS ROLE in 9/11 ATTACK

bers of the Jemaah Islamiyya terrorist organization, a Southeast Asian-based terrorist network with links to al-Qa'ida.

- On May 12 and November 9, 2003, al-Qa'ida operatives conducted bombings of residential compounds that housed Western workers in Riyadh, Saudi Arabia. The first incident claimed dozens of lives and injured nearly 200 others. The second resulted in 18 deaths and over 120 injuries.

- On May 16, 2003, five nearly simultaneous explosions in Casablanca, Morocco, killed 41 people and injured approximately 100 others. Although no definitive evidence links al-Qa'ida to the bombings in Casablanca, the Sunni extremist group responsible for this attack may have al-Qa'ida ties.

- On March 11, 2004, a series of 10 bombs detonated on four commuter trains in Madrid, Spain. The near simultaneous explosions killed 191 people and injured more than 1,400 others. Spanish police have traced responsibility for the attack to Moroccan Islamic militants with ties to al-Qa'ida.

- On July 7, 2005, four coordinated bomb blasts struck London's public transit system during the morning rush hour. Fifty-two people were killed and approximately 700 injured in the attack, including the death of one American and the wounding of four others. The London bombing was distinctive in having involved "homegrown" jihadist terrorists operating in a Western, predominantly non-Muslim country.

The use of WMD against civilian targets represents the most serious potential international and domestic terrorism threat facing the United States today and provides a glimpse into emerging terrorist scenarios of the 21st century. A variety of intelligence reporting indicates that al-Qa'ida has energetically sought to acquire and experiment with biological, chemical, and radiological weapons of mass destruction. The January 2003 arrests in the United Kingdom of Algerian extremists suspected of producing the biological toxin ricin exemplifies the interest some Islamic militants have in the operational use of such agents. In April 2004, Jordanian authorities disrupted a plot by Islamic extremists to generate a cloud of cyanide gas in Amman.

Ricin and the bacterial agent anthrax are emerging as the most prevalent agents involved in WMD investigations. Prior to the fall of 2001, there had been no criminal cases involving the actual use of anthrax in the United States. In September and October of that year, however, several anthrax-tainted letters were received in Florida, New York, New Jersey, Connecticut, and the District of Columbia. The contaminations resulted in five fatalities and 22 infections. On February 2, 2004, in an incident for which no threat was made or threat letter identified, ricin was discovered on the automated mail opening system used in the Washington, D.C., office of U.S. Senate Majority Leader William Frist. Both the anthrax mailings of 2001 and the 2004 ricin incident remain under investigation by the FBI, and their connection to domestic or international terrorism has not been determined.

JUNE 21, 2002	JULY 2002	SEPTEMBER 13-14, 2002	OCTOBER 4, 2002
CREATION of the FBI FLY TEAM	CREATION of the NATIONAL JOINT TERRORISM TASK FORCE	ARREST of LACKAWANNA SIX TERROR CELL MEMBERS	JOHN WALKER LINDH SENTENCED to 20 YEARS in PRISON after PLEADING GUILTY to TERRORISM CHARGES

LEGISLATIVE ACTION

In his September 20, 2001, address to a Joint Session of Congress and the American people, President Bush declared a war to disrupt global terrorism, beginning with al-Qa'ida. The war on terrorism has included military action to overthrow Afghanistan's Taliban government and Sadaam Hussein's Baathist regime in Iraq, as well as a multifaceted campaign involving diplomacy, economic sanctions, covert intelligence operations, and law enforcement action. In the weeks immediately following the September 11, 2001, attack, Congress and the President enacted legislation and policies intended to minimize the possibility of another catastrophic act of terrorism from occurring on U.S. soil.

On October 26, 2001, Congress passed the Uniting and Strengthening America by Providing Appropriate Tools Required to Interrupt and Obstruct Terrorism Act of 2001 (USA PATRIOT Act), which includes changes to national security authorities, criminal and immigration laws, and money-laundering and victim assistance statutes. In making these modifications to existing laws, Congress intended to strengthen the capabilities of federal law enforcement in the fight against terrorism while simultaneously protecting civil liberties. The USA PATRIOT Act improved the processes by which federal law enforcement officials obtain legal authority for conducting surveillance and allowed for greater information sharing between criminal investigators and intelligence collectors. The act modified the definition of terrorism as a federal crime to include several offenses likely to be committed by terrorists, including certain computer crimes and a number of violent crimes involving aircraft. New federal offenses include attacks on mass transportation systems, vehicles, facilities, or passengers; harboring or concealing persons who have committed or are about to commit an act of terrorism; expansion of the prohibition against providing material support or resources to terrorists; and possessing a biological agent or toxin of a type or in a quantity that is not reasonably justified for specifically defined purposes. Additionally, the inclusion of the International Money Laundering Abatement and Financial Anti-Terrorism Act of 2001 into the USA PATRIOT Act significantly increased the United States' ability to combat the financing of terrorism.

On October 29, 2001, President Bush issued Homeland Security Presidential Directive No. 2 (HSPD-2). Among its provisions, HSPD-2 offers federal guidance for keeping foreign terrorists and their supporters out of the United States through entry denial, removal, and prosecution.

On November 27, 2002, Congress and the President created the National Commission on Terrorist Attacks Upon the United States (Public Law 107-306) with a mandate "to investigate 'facts and circumstances relating to the terrorist attacks of September 11, 2001,' including those relating to intelligence agencies, law enforcement agencies, diplomacy, immigration issues and border control, the flow of assets to terrorist organizations, commercial aviation, the role of congressional oversight and resource allocation," and other relevant areas.[11]

[11] National Commission on Terrorist Attacks Upon the United States, *The 9/11 Commission Report* (New York: W.W. Norton & Co., 2004), preface, xv.

OCTOBER 12, 2002	NOVEMBER 8, 2002	NOVEMBER 25, 2002
JEMAAH ISLAMIYYA BOMBING OF NIGHTCLUB in BALI, INDONESIA 202 killed	SYMBIONESE LIBERATION ARMY MEMBER JAMES WILLIAM KILGORE ARRESTED in CAPE TOWN, SOUTH AFRICA	HOMELAND SECURITY ACT OF 2002 OFFICIALLY ESTABLISHES the U.S. DEPARTMENT of HOMELAND SECURITY

On July 22, 2004, the 9/11 Commission published a summary of its investigative findings along with recommendations designed to guard against future attacks. In response to this report, President Bush signed into law on December 8 the Intelligence Reform and Terrorism Prevention Act of 2004 (IRTPA). This act instituted reforms to FISA and modifications to material support statutes for prosecuting terrorists. The IRTPA also created the Office of the Director of National Intelligence and established the Director of National Intelligence (DNI) as the head of the U.S. Intelligence Community. In addition, the act created the National Counter Proliferation Center to oversee the Intelligence Community's efforts against the proliferation of weapons of mass destruction; the Joint Intelligence Community Council to assist the DNI in establishing a collective national intelligence effort; the Privacy and Civil Liberties Oversight Board within the Executive Office; and instituted the joint-agency National Counterterrorism Center as the primary entity for analyzing intelligence pertaining to transnational terrorism.

FBI INITIATIVES

Director Robert S. Mueller III (2001-present) took office in the FBI on September 4, 2001, with an agenda to restructure the Bureau and upgrade its technology. Seven days later, the September 11 terrorist attack gave greater urgency to this agenda and focused it on the prevention of future terrorist attacks. On May 29, 2002, Director Mueller formally elevated counterterrorism and the prevention of future terrorist attacks against U.S. interests to the FBI's preeminent mission. In response to this mandate, the FBI moved away from its traditional field-oriented approach to setting priorities and managing cases, to a more centralized national approach in which counterterrorism was the overriding priority in every field office and all international counterterrorism cases were managed centrally by FBI Headquarters. The shift of resources to meet this new priority has resulted in a significant structural reorganization at the FBI that includes a greatly expanded counterterrorism program.

MARCH 1, 2003	MARCH 20, 2003	MAY 12, 2003
KHALID SHEIK MOHAMMED, AL-QA'IDA OPERATIONAL COMMANDER and MASTERMIND of 9/11 ATTACK CAPTURED in PAKISTAN	UNITED STATES and COALITION PARTNERS BEGIN MILITARY ACTION in IRAQ	BOMBING of RESIDENTIAL COMPOUNDS in RIYADH, SAUDI ARABIA

FBI PRIORITIES

Three factors influence the ranking of priorities: the significance of the threat to the security of the United States; the priority the American public places upon the threat; and the degree to which addressing the threat falls most exclusively within the FBI's jurisdiction. In executing the following priorities, the FBI produces and uses intelligence to protect the nation from threats and to bring to justice those who violate the law.

1. Protect the United States from terrorist attack.
2. Protect the United States against foreign intelligence operations and espionage.
3. Protect the United States against cyber-based attacks and high-technology crimes.
4. Combat public corruption at all levels.
5. Protect civil rights.
6. Combat transnational and national criminal organizations and enterprises.
7. Combat major white-collar crime.
8. Combat significant violent crime.
9. Support federal, state, municipal, and international partners.
10. Upgrade technology to successfully perform the FBI's mission.

As the top priority, counterterrorism receives first consideration throughout the Bureau in the allocation of funding, physical space, resources, and the hiring and training of personnel.

The current shape of the Counterterrorism Division reflects the complexity of terrorism as the United States currently faces it, with branches, sections, and units that focus upon domestic terrorism, different global regions of international terrorist activity, and terrorists' methods of operation, finance, and communication. This reorganization supports the Bureau's current strategic mission of preventing terrorist attacks while preserving the civil liberties of all American citizens. This strategic mission also identifies the Bureau's law enforcement and domestic intelligence leadership roles within the U.S. Intelligence Community. In these leadership capacities, the FBI defines the domestic and international terrorism threats to the Homeland, contributes to the Intelligence Community in its evaluation of those threats, and provides investigative and crisis response in the event a terrorist attack does occur. Many of the organizational changes, developments in strategic mission, and the initiatives discussed below anticipated the recommendations made in July 2004, when the 9/11 Commission published its endorsement of the FBI's continuing role in terrorism prevention and urged the Bureau to institutionalize and cultivate its expertise in intelligence and national security.[12]

[12] National Commission on Terrorist Attacks upon the United States, *The 9/11 Commission Report*, 423-27.

MAY 31, 2003	AUGUST 5, 2003	FEBRUARY 9, 2004
ERIC ROBERT RUDOLPH ARRESTED and CHARGED in CONNECTION to SEVERAL BOMBINGS, INCLUDING a BOMBING at CENTENNIAL OLYMPIC PARK in ATLANTA, GEORGIA	JEMAAH ISLAMIYYA BOMBING of JW MARRIOTT HOTEL in JAKARTA, INDONESIA 11 killed	FINAL SENTENCING in PORTLAND TERROR CELL CASE

FOCUS ON PREVENTION

One of the most effective weapons in the prevention of terrorist attacks involves the gathering, analysis, and dissemination of intelligence and the full integration of that intelligence into investigations, operations, and crisis response. To this end, in December 2001, the FBI merged the counterterrorism analytical activities of the Investigative Services Division into the Counterterrorism Division and established the Office of Intelligence to cultivate the division's analytical workforce and develop information-sharing policies. In response to the IRTPA and a subsequent Presidential directive, the FBI redesignated the Office of Intelligence as the Directorate of Intelligence and, in September 2005, incorporated it into the newly created National Security Branch, which oversees all of the Bureau's national intelligence programs, projects, activities, and workforce.

Domestically through its field offices, and internationally through its Legat offices, the FBI has a significant infrastructure in place by which to gather intelligence. Although the FBI has traditionally employed its intelligence analysts in "tactical," or case-specific support capacities, the mandate to prevent acts of terrorism has led the FBI to develop a professional corps of analysts who study broader terrorism trends and assess priority threats at the "strategic," or predictive, level. In 2002, the Counterterrorism Division established an Analytical Branch to develop actionable and strategic intelligence for FBI field offices, the U.S. Intelligence Community, and domestic and international law enforcement partners. In September 2003, the FBI established Field Intelligence Groups in each of its field offices to analyze and direct the collection of information, and ensure its appropriate dissemination.

FOCUS ON PARTNERSHIPS

The timely two-way flow of information between appropriate federal, state, and local partners is a key element in dismantling terrorist organizations and eliminating threats. Whereas the primary consumer of FBI intelligence used to be its field offices, FBI agents and analysts now regularly communicate with the larger U.S. Intelligence Community and other federal agencies, law enforcement partners at the state and local levels, and private and public sectors of society. At the federal level, a new, multi-agency National Joint Terrorism Task Force (NJTTF) was integrated into the Counterterrorism Division at FBI Headquarters in June 2002. Staffed by representatives from more than 40 federal, state, and local agencies, the NJTTF coordinates the flow of information between its participating entities and over 100 JTTFs that were in place nationwide by the end of 2005. In addition, the FBI details agents and analysts to numerous federal agencies, including the CIA, National Security Agency, National Security Council, Defense Intelligence Agency, Department of Homeland Security, and the National Counterterrorism Center (NCTC).[13]

[13] The Terrorist Threat Integration Center (TTIC) was established by presidential directive and became operational on May 1, 2003. NCTC replaced TTIC on December 6, 2004.

MARCH 11, 2004	JULY 22, 2004	SEPTEMBER 29, 2004	DECEMBER 8, 2004
BOMBINGS of the MADRID TRANSIT SYSTEM 191 killed approximately 1700 wounded	The NATIONAL COMMISSION on TERRORIST ATTACKS UPON the UNITED STATES PUBLISHES *The 9/11 COMMISSION REPORT*	SENTENCING in *USS COLE* BOMBING	INTELLIGENCE REFORM and TERRORISM PREVENTION ACT SIGNED into LAW

In response to HSPD-2, the Attorney General established the Foreign Terrorist Tracking Task Force (FTTTF) to track and identify terrorists and, on August 6, 2002, consolidated the task force into the FBI. In addition to its federal agency participants, the FTTTF maintains a close liaison with foreign intelligence and law enforcement services. In another terrorist tracking initiative, on September 16, 2003, the President directed the Attorney General, Secretary of Homeland Security, Secretary of State, and Director of Central Intelligence to develop the Terrorist Screening Center (TSC) to consolidate information from terrorist watch lists and provide 24-hour, seven-day-a-week operational support for law enforcement, consular officers, and other officials. The TSC began operations on December 1, 2003.

An example of interagency cooperation led by the FBI involves the analysis of improvised explosive devices (IEDs)—a technology used in most of the terrorist attacks against U.S. citizens and interests during the past five years. These explosives often reflect the unique characteristics, or signature, of the terrorist organizations or individuals who made them. In December 2003 the FBI Laboratory began preliminary operations of the Terrorist Explosive Device Analytical Center (TEDAC) to coordinate and manage a national effort to gather and analyze information on IEDs recovered both inside and outside the United States. TEDAC uses the knowledge gained from its analysis to assist in the investigation of terrorist bombing attacks, to develop countermeasures to defeat IEDs, and to train first-responders in terrorist IED techniques.

Shortly after the events of September 11, 2001, the FBI undertook several initiatives to integrate state and local law enforcement into counterterrorism operations. On February 27, 2002, the Counterterrorism Division issued its first weekly FBI Intelligence Bulletin to provide actionable terrorism-related intelligence to law enforcement partners. The Bulletin currently reaches more than 60 federal agencies, all FBI field offices and Legats, and more than 18,000 state and local law enforcement agencies through secure communication systems.[14] Since September 11, 2001, the Counterterrorism Division has also disseminated Intelligence Assessments and several thousand Information Intelligence Reports to the U.S. Intelligence Community and appropriate state and local law enforcement entities. In spring 2002 the FBI created the Office of Law Enforcement Coordination (OLEC) as a liaison between the Bureau and other law enforcement organizations. In response to a USA PATRIOT Act mandate, the FBI has participated with other federal agencies in the State and Local Anti-Terrorism Training initiative (SLATT), which has raised the level of counterterrorism expertise and developed professional relationships among law enforcement partners.

[14] Beginning on August 6, 2004, the FBI began routinely disseminating bulletins jointly with the U.S. Department of Homeland Security.

APRIL 6, 2005	APRIL 24, 2005	APRIL 26, 2005
CREATIVITY LEADER MATTHEW HALE SENTENCED to 40 YEARS IN PRISON for SOLICITATION of VIOLENCE and OBSTRUCTION of JUSTICE	ZACARIAS MOUSSAOUI PLEADS GUILTY to SIX CHARGES in CONNECTION to the 9/11 attack	ALI AL-TIMIMI, SPIRITUAL LEADER of the "VIRGINIA JIHAD" GROUP, CONVICTED on TERRORISM CHARGES

GLOBAL FOCUS

The investigation into the September 11, 2001, attack—which at its height involved more than 7,000 FBI agents and support personnel, including approximately 700 personnel deployed overseas—underscored the global nature of terrorism and the ability of terrorists to plan, finance, and conduct operations in a variety of countries around the world. The transition in recent decades from terrorism as a primarily domestic concern to one of global implications has led the FBI to develop its intelligence and law enforcement partnerships worldwide.

This has led to new initiatives and the cultivation of old ones, including the continued expansion of the Legat program and the offering of counterterrorism training to international law enforcement agencies at the National Academy at Quantico and International Law Enforcement Academies in Budapest, Hungary; Bangkok, Thailand; and Gaborone, Botswana. Other venues of international cooperation include FBI participation in the Group of 8, the Organization of American States, the NATO alliance, and chairing the International Association of Chiefs of Police Committee on Terrorism.

In October 2001 the FBI established a Most Wanted Terrorists List to engage the international public's assistance in the war on terrorism. Set at 22 names, this list places a "global spotlight" on indicted terrorist suspects. Those who initially occupied the list took part in the 1985 hijacking of TWA flight 847, the 1993 World Trade Center bombing, the "Manila Air" plot, the bombing of Khobar Towers, and the U.S. embassy bombings in East Africa. Usama Bin Ladin occupies a place on this list and on that of the FBI's list of Top Ten Most Wanted Fugitives.

CONCLUSION

During the first 75 years of its history the FBI encountered a predominantly domestic terrorist threat that underlay larger criminal trends. Between the World Wars, this threat came primarily from right-wing extremists, then shifted to left-wing, socialist-oriented groups beginning in the 1950s and continuing into the 1980s. In the early 1980s, international terrorism–sponsored primarily by states or organizations–began to impact US interests overseas and led to legislation that extended the FBI's responsibilities to cover terrorist threats originating outside the United States and its territories. The 1990s saw a new era of domestic and international terrorism in which terrorists sought to inflict massive and indiscriminate casualties upon civilian populations. This threat grew as terrorists began to seek out unconventional weapons and weapons of mass destruction. The 1990s also saw the rise of terrorism pursued by loosely-affiliated extremists, with examples ranging from terrorists involved with domestic special interest causes to militants engaged in international jihad. These terrorism trends combined into the September 11, 2001, attack that has set in motion an international effort to counter the global terrorist threat and elevated counterterrorism to the FBI's preeminent mission.

JULY 7, 2005	JULY 18, 2005	AUGUST 30, 2005
BOMBINGS of the LONDON TRANSIT SYSTEM 52 killed approximately 700 injured	ERIC ROBERT RUDOLPH SENTENCED to LIFE in PRISON	SEAN GILLESPIE SENTENCED to 39 YEARS for FIREBOMBING a SYNAGOGUE in 2004

In his September 20, 2001, Address to a Joint Session of Congress and the American People, President Bush assured his audience that in the present conflict with terrorism, violence would be met with "patient justice." The struggle against terrorism—especially that currently waged against al-Qa'ida—is one of endurance, and it is one in which the FBI is prepared to engage with unflagging persistence. Although the preeminent mission of protecting the United States from terrorist attack is changing the character of the FBI as a whole, an abiding strength of the FBI remains its tradition of excellence in vigorously investigating and prosecuting criminal acts. These traditional pursuits are essential to the disruption of terrorist activities, the dismantling of terrorist organizations, and, consequently, the prevention of future terrorist attacks. By combining a willingness to innovate with its traditional law enforcement responsibilities, the FBI continues to evolve in order to counter the varied forms of terrorism that threaten the interests and security of the United States.

UPDATES

To ensure that the most current terrorism-related information is available to the American public, the FBI continually evaluates, and, when investigation warrants, updates terrorism statistics presented in the *Terrorism* series. In this issue, the following two acts, which were committed during 1998 and 1999, have been added to the concluding chronological summary of terrorist incidents.

JUNE 27, 1998
Oso Complex Fire
Espanola, New Mexico
(One act of Domestic Terrorism)

On June 27, 1998, a wildfire originated by arson began in the Espanola Ranger District, 10 miles northwest of Espanola, New Mexico. Known as the Oso Complex Fire, the blaze reached within eight miles of Los Alamos and burned a total of 5,185 forested acres, including on Santa Fe National Forest and Santa Clara Pueblo lands. The cost to suppress the fire was $3,433,983. In November 1998, the Albuquerque Journal received a letter claiming the wildfire on behalf of a local militia group, the Minutemen, as a statement against the killing of gray wolves. Associates of the group are suspected of arsons and threats targeting federal and state land use and environmental advocacy groups over apparent disagreements with environmental causes during the late 1990s.

MARCH 19, 1999
Pipe Bombing
Santa Fe, New Mexico
(One act of Domestic Terrorism)

On March 19, 1999, a pipe bomb improvised explosive device (IED) was discovered in a mailbox at Forest Guardians in Santa Fe, New Mexico. The pipe bomb failed to detonate apparently because the cigarette intended to initiate the IED burned out before igniting the fuse. Forest Guardians is a nonprofit group devoted to stopping commercial logging in national forests, and other environmental issues.

On February 14, 2003, law enforcement officers with the FBI, U.S. Forest Service, and Espanola, New Mexico Police arrested Raymond Anthony Sandoval for setting the June 27, 1998, Oso Complex Fire and the attempted March 19, 1999, Forest Guardians bombing. On June 25, 2003, Sandoval pled guilty to manufacturing a destructive device, possession of an unregistered firearm, arson on federal land, and willfully injuring property of the United States. On October 7, 2003, Sandoval, was sentenced to 84 months incarceration and ordered to make restitution payment of $3 million.

The following Chronological Summary includes all of the terrorist incidents recorded in the *Terrorism/Terrorism in the United States* series. The statistical information contained in the following summary supports the graphs and charts presented in this publication.

CHRONOLOGICAL SUMMARY OF
TERRORIST INCIDENTS IN THE UNITED STATES 1980-2005

DATE	LOCATION	INCIDENT TYPE	PERPETRATOR	KILLED	INJURED
1-7-80	San Juan, PR	Pipe Bombing	Anti-Communist Alliance		
1-13-80	New York, NY	Bombing	Omega 7		4
1-13-80	Miami, FL	Bombing	Omega 7		
1-19-80	San Juan, PR	Bombing	Omega 7		
3-12-80	Hato Rey, PR	Armed Assault	Ejercito Popular Boricua Macheteros		
3-15-80	Chicago, IL	Hostile Takeovers (2)	Armed Forces of National Liberation		
3-17-80	New York, NY	Bombing	Croatian Freedom Fighters		3
3-25-80	New York, NY	Attempted Bombing	Omega 7		
4-19-80	Chattanooga, TN	Shooting	Justice Knights of the Ku Klux Klan		4
4-30-80	New York, NY	Assault	Revolutionary Communist Party		
6-3-80	Washington, DC	Bombing	Croatian Freedom Fighters		
6-3-80	New York, NY	Bombing	Croatian Freedom Fighters		
7-14-80	Dorato, PR San Juan, PR	Multiple Bombings (2)	Organization of Volunteers for the Puerto Rico Revolution		
7-14-80	Ponce, PR Mayaguez, PR	Multiple Arsons (2)	Organization of Volunteers for the Puerto Rico Revolution		
7-22-80	Hato Rey, PR Santurce, PR Rio Piedras, PR	Multiple Bombings (4)	Revolutionary Commandos of the People, Ready and at War		
8-20-80	Berkeley, CA	Pipe Bombing	Iranian Free Army		2
9-11-80	New York, NY	Shooting	Omega 7	1	
10-7-80	New York, NY	Attempted Bombing	International Committee Against Nazism		
10-12-80	New York, NY	Bombing	Justice Commandos of the Armenian Genocide		4
10-12-80	Hollywood, CA	Bombing	Justice Commandos of the Armenian Genocide		1
10-14-80	Fort Collins, CO	Shooting	Libyan Revolutionary Committee		1
12-21-80	New York, NY	Pipe Bombing	Armed Forces of Popular Resistance		
12-30-80	Hialeah, FL	Attempted Bombing	Omega 7		
1-8-81	Santurce, PR Ponce, PR Rio Piedras, PR	Multiple Incendiary Bombings (3)	People's Revolutionary Commandos		
1-12-81	San Juan, PR	Bombing	Ejercito Popular Boricua Macheteros		
1-23-81	New York City, NY	Bombing	Croatian Freedom Fighters		

CHRONOLOGICAL SUMMARY OF
TERRORIST INCIDENTS IN THE UNITED STATES 1980-2005

DATE	LOCATION	INCIDENT TYPE	PERPETRATOR	KILLED	INJURED
1-26-81	San Francisco, CA	Bombing	Jewish Defense League/American Revenge Committee		
2-2-81	Los Angeles, CA	Attempted Bombing	October 3		
2-9-81	Eugene, OR	Assault	Revolutionary Communist Youth Brigade		
2-22-81	Hollywood, CA	Bombing	Armenian Secret Army for the Liberation of Armenia		
3-15-81	San Juan, PR	Attempted Bombing	Armed Forces of Popular Resistance		
4-21-81	Santurce, PR	Robbery	Ejercito Popular Boricua Macheteros		
4-27-81	Washington, DC	Incendiary Bombing	Iranian Patriotic Army		
5/16-18/81	New York City, NY	Multiple Bombings (5)	Puerto Rican Armed Resistance	1	
6-25-81	Torrance, CA	Incendiary Bombing	Jewish Defenders		
6-26-81	Los Angeles, CA	Bombing	June 9 Organization		
7-30-81	New York City, NY	Hostile Takeover	Libyan Students		
8-7-81	Washington, DC	Hostile Takeover	People's Mujahedin Organization of Iran		3
8-20-81	Washington, DC	Arson	Black Brigade		
8-20-81	Los Angeles, CA	Bombing	June 9 Organization		
8-27-81	Carolina, PR	Bombing	Grupo Estrella		
8-31-81	New York City, NY	Hostile Takeover	Jewish Defense League		
9/3-4/81	New York City, NY	Multiple Bombings (2)	Jewish Defense League		
9-9-81	Washington, DC	Assault	Concerned Sierra Leone Nationals		
9-11-81	Miami, FL	Multiple Bombings (2)	Omega 7		
9-12-81	New York City, NY	Bombing	Omega 7		
9-22-81	Schenectady, NY	Bombing	Communist Workers Party		
9-24-81	Miami, FL	Attempted Bombing	Omega 7		
10-1-81	Hollywood, CA	Bombing	Armenian Secret Army for the Liberation of Armenia		
10-25-81	New York City, NY	Incendiary Bombing	Jewish Defense League		
11-11-81	Santurce, PR	Bombing	Ejercito Popular Boricua Macheteros		
11-14-81	Glen Cove, NY	Shooting	Unaffiliated Extremists		
11-20-81	Los Angeles, CA	Bombing	Justice Commandos of the Armenian Genocide		
11-27-81	Fort Buchanan, PR	Shooting	National Liberation Movement		1
11-27-81	Santurce, PR Condado, PR	Multiple Bombings (2)	Ejercito Popular Boricua Macheteros		
12-24-81	New York City, NY	Attempted Pipe Bombing	Jewish Defense League		

CHRONOLOGICAL SUMMARY OF
TERRORIST INCIDENTS IN THE UNITED STATES 1980-2005

DATE	LOCATION	INCIDENT TYPE	PERPETRATOR	KILLED	INJURED
1-28-82	Los Angeles, CA	Shooting	Justice Commandos of the Armenian Genocide	1	
2-19-82	Miami, FL	Multiple Bombings (2)	Omega 7		
2-19-82	Washington, DC	Bombing	Jewish Defense League		
2-21-82	Rio Piedras, PR	Pipe Bombing	Antonia Martinez Student Commandos		
2-28-82	New York City, NY	Multiple Bombings (4)	Armed Forces of National Liberation		
3-22-82	Cambridge, MA	Bombing	Justice Commandos of the Armenian Genocide		
4-5-82	Brooklyn, NY	Arson	Jewish Defense League	1	7
4-28-82	New York City, NY	Multiple Bombings (2)	Jewish Defense League		
4-29-82	San Juan, PR Bayamon, PR	Multiple Bombings (2)	Provisional Coordinating Committee of the Labor Self-Defense Group		
4-29-82	San Juan, PR	Shooting	Provisional Coordinating Committee of the Labor Self-Defense Group		
5-4-82	Somerville, MA	Shooting	Justice Commandos of the Armenian Genocide	1	
5-16-82	San Juan, PR	Shooting	Ejercito Popular Boricua Macheteros/ Group for the Liberation of Vieques	1	3
5-17-82	Union City, NJ	Incendiary Bombing	Omega 7		
5-19-82	Villa Sin Miedo, PR	Shooting	Ejercito Popular Boricua Macheteros	1	12
5-20-82	San Juan, PR	Attempted Bombing	Ejercito Popular Boricua Macheteros		
5-25-82	San German, PR	Kidnapping	Grupo Estrella		1
5-30-82	Van Nuys, CA	Attempted Bombing	Armenian Secret Army for the Liberation of Armenia		
6-10-82	Carolina, PR	Multiple Bombings (3)	Armed Forces of Popular Resistance		
7-4-82	New York City, NY Astoria, NY	Multiple Pipe Bombings (2)	Croatian Freedom Fighters		
7-5-82	New York City, NY	Multiple Pipe Bombings (2)	Jewish Defense League		
8-20-82	Old San Juan, PR	Bombing	Armed Forces of National Liberation		
9-1-82	Naranjito, PR	Attempted Bombing	Ejercito Popular Boricua Macheteros		
9-2-82	Miami, FL	Bombing	Omega 7		
9-8-82	Chicago, IL	Bombing	Omega 7		
9-20-82	New York City, NY	Bombing	Armed Forces of National Liberation		
9-25-82	Miami, FL	Attempted Bombing	Omega 7		
10-15-82	Washington, DC	Hostile Takeover	Islamic Extremists		
10-22-82	Philadelphia, PA	Attempted Bombing	Justice Commandos of the Armenian Genocide		

CHRONOLOGICAL SUMMARY OF
TERRORIST INCIDENTS IN THE UNITED STATES 1980-2005

DATE	LOCATION	INCIDENT TYPE	PERPETRATOR	KILLED	INJURED
11-4-82	New York City, NY	Smoke Bombing	Jewish Defense League		
11-16-82	Carolina, PR	Multiple Robberies (2)	Ejercito Popular Boricua Macheteros	1	
12-8-82	Washington, DC	Attempted Bombing	Norman David Mayer	1	
12-16-82	Elmont, NY	Multiple Bombings (2)	United Freedom Front		
12-21-82	New York City, NY	Attempted Pipe Bombing	Jewish Defense League		
12-22-82	McLean, VA	Hostile Takeover	People of Omar		
12-31-82	New York City, NY	Multiple Bombings (5)	Armed Forces of National Liberation		3
1/11-12/83	Miami, FL	Multiple Bombings (3)	Omega 7		
1-28-83	New York City, NY	Bombing	Revolutionary Fighting Group		
2-13-83	Medina, ND	Shooting	Sheriff's Posse Comitatus	2	4
2-15-83	Killeen, TX	Hijacking	Hossein Olya		
2-19-83	Washington, DC	Pipe Bombing	Jewish Defense League		
3-20-83	San Antonio, TX	Bombing	Republic of Revolutionary		
4-26-83	Washington, DC	Bombing	Armed Resistance Unit		
4-27-83	Miami, FL	Attempted Bombings (4)	Haitian Extremists		
4-29-83	Rio Piedras, PR	Hostile Takeover	Ejercito Popluar Boricua Macheteros		
5-12-83	Uniondale, NY	Bombing	United Freedom Front		
5-13-83	New York City, NY	Bombing	United Freedom Front		
5-27-83	Miami, FL	Bombing	Omega 7		
7-8-83	Miami, FL	Kidnapping	Ejercito Revolucionario Del Pueblo		
7-15-83	Rio Piedras, PR	Robbery	Ejercito Popular Boricua Macheteros	1	
8-8-83	Detroit, MI	Attempted Incendiary Bombing	Fuqra		
8-8-83	Detroit, MI	Shooting	Fuqra	1	
8-9-83	Detroit, MI	Arson	Fuqra	2	
8-16-83	Los Angeles, CA	Hostile Takeover	Carlos Martinez		
8-18-83	Washington, DC	Bombing	Armed Resistance Unit		
8-21-83	New York City, NY	Bombing	United Freedom Front		
8-27-83	Washington, DC	Incendiary Bombing	Unknown		
10-12-83	Miami, FL	Pipe Bombing	Omega 7		
10-30-83	Hato Rey, PR	Rocket Attack	Ejercito Popular Boricua Macheteros		
11-7-83	Washington, DC	Bombing	Armed Resistance Unit		

CHRONOLOGICAL SUMMARY OF
TERRORIST INCIDENTS IN THE UNITED STATES 1980-2005

DATE	LOCATION	INCIDENT TYPE	PERPETRATOR	KILLED	INJURED
12/13-14/83	East Meadow, NY New York City, NY	Multiple Bombings (2)	United Freedom Front		
1-29-84	New York City, NY	Bombing	United Freedom Front		
2-23-84	New York City, NY	Bombing	Jewish Direct Action		
3-19-84	Harrison, NY	Bombing	United Freedom Front		
4-5-84	New York City, NY	Bombing	Red Guerrilla Resistance		
4-20-84	Washington, DC	Bombing	Red Guerrilla Resistance		
5-9-84	New York City, NY	Attempted Assassination	Bashir Baesho		
8-22-84	Melville, NY	Bombing	United Freedom Front		
9-26-84	New York City, NY	Bombing	Red Guerrilla Resistance		
9-26-84	Mount Pleasant, NY	Bombing	United Freedom Front		
12-10-84	Levittown, PR Rio Piedras, PR Ponce, PR Mayaguez, PR Cayey, PR	Multiple Bombings (5)	Organization of Volunteers for the Puerto Rican Revolution		
1-25-85	Old San Juan, PR	Rocket Attack	Ejercito Popular Boricua Macheteros/ Organization of Volunteers for the Puerto Rican Revolution		
2-23-85	New York City, NY	Bombing	Red Guerrilla Resistance		
5-15-85	Northridge, CA	Pipe Bombing	Jewish Defense League		
8-15-85	Paterson, NJ	Bombing	Jewish Defense League	1	1
9-6-85	Brentwood, NY	Bombing	Jewish Defense League		1
10-11-85	Santa Ana, CA	Bombing	Jewish Defense League	1	7
11-6-85	Bayamon, PR	Shooting	Organization of Volunteers for the Puerto Rican Revolution		1
1-6-86	Cidra, PR Toa Baja, PR Guanica, PR Santurce, PR	Multiple Bombings (4)	Ejercito Revolucionario Clandestino/ National Revolutionary Front of Puerto Rico		
3-17-86	Ponce, PR	Attempted Bombing	Commando Rojo		
4-14-86	Rio Piedras, PR	Bombing	Organization of Volunteers for the Puerto Rican Revolution		
4-29-86	San Juan, PR	Shooting	Organization of Volunteers for the Puerto Rican Revolution	1	1
5-14-86	Phoenix, AZ	Sabotage	Earth First Organization		
9-2-86	New York City, NY	Tear Gas Bombing	Jewish Defense League		17
9-15-86	Coeur d'Alene, ID	Pipe Bombing	Aryan Nations		

CHRONOLOGICAL SUMMARY OF
TERRORIST INCIDENTS IN THE UNITED STATES 1980-2005

DATE	LOCATION	INCIDENT TYPE	PERPETRATOR	KILLED	INJURED
9-29-86	Coeur d'Alene, ID	Multiple Bombings (4)	Aryan Nations		
10-20-86	New York City, NY	Incendiary Bombing	Jewish Defense League		
10-28-86	Bayamon, PR Fajardo, PR Mayaguez, PR Aguadilla, PR Santurce, PR Fort Buchanan, PR	Multiple Bombings (7)	Ejercito Popular Boricua Macheteros		1
11-4-86	Puerta De Tierra, PR	Attempted Bombing	Ejercito Popular Boricua Macheteros		
12-28-86	Yauco, PR Guayama, PR	Multiple Bombings (2)	Ejercito Popular Boricua Macheteros		
4-16-87	Davis, CA	Arson	Animal Liberation Front		
5-25-87	Caguas, PR Carolina, PR Mayaguez, PR Cidra, PR Aibonita, PR Ponce, PR	Multiple Bombings (7)	Guerrilla Forces of Liberation		
11-9-87	Flagstaff, AZ	Sabotage	Evan Mecham Eco-Terrorist International Conspiracy		
1-12-88	Rio Piedras, PR	Multiple Incendiary Bombings (2)	Pedro Albizu Campos Revolutionary Forces		
5-26-88	Coral Gables, FL	Bombing	Organization Alliance of Cuban Intransigence		
7-22-88	Caguas, PR	Pipe Bombing	Ejercito Popular Boricua Macheteros		
9-19-88	Los Angeles, CA	Bombing	Up the IRS, Inc.		
9-25-88	Grand Canyon, AZ	Sabotage	Evan Mecham Eco-Terrorist International Conspiracy		
10-25-88	Flagstaff, AZ	Sabotage	Evan Mecham Eco-Terrorist International Conspiracy		
11-1-88	Rio Piedras, PR	Multiple Bombings (2)	Pedro Albizu Campos Revolutionary Forces		
4-3-89	Tucson, AZ	Arson	Animal Liberation Front		
6-19-89	Bayamon, PR	Multiple Bombings (2)	Ejercito Popular Boricua Macheteros		
7/3-4/89	Lubbock, TX	Malicious Destruction of Property	Animal Liberation Front		
1-12-90	Santurce, PR Carolina, PR	Multiple Pipe Bombings (2)	Eugenio Maria de Hostos International Brigade of the Pedro Albizu Campos Revolutionary Forces		

CHRONOLOGICAL SUMMARY OF
TERRORIST INCIDENTS IN THE UNITED STATES 1980-2005

DATE	LOCATION	INCIDENT TYPE	PERPETRATOR	KILLED	INJURED
2-22-90	Los Angeles, CA	Bombing	Up the IRS, Inc.		
4-22-90	Santa Cruz County, CA	Malicious Destruction of Property	Earth Night Action Group		
5-27-90	Mayaguez, PR	Arson	Unknown Puerto Rican Group		
9-17-90	Arecibo, PR Vega Baja, PR	Multiple Bombings (2)	Pedro Albizu Group Revolutionary Forces		
2-3-91	Mayaguez, PR	Arson	Popular Liberation Army		
2-18-91	Sabana Grande, PR	Arson	Popular Liberation Army		
3-17-91	Carolina, PR	Arson	Unknown Puerto Rican Group		
4-1-91	Fresno, CA	Bombing	Popular Liberation Army		
7-6-91	Punta Borinquen, PR	Bombing	Popular Liberation Army		
4-5-92	New York, NY	Hostile Takeover	Mujahedin-E-Khalq		
11-19-92	Urbana, IL	Attempted Firebombing	Mexican Revolutionary Movement		
12-10-92	Chicago, IL	Car Fire and Attempted Firebombing (2)	Boricua Revolutionary Front		
2-26-93	New York, NY	Car Bombing	International Islamist Extremists	6	1042
7/20-22/93	Tacoma, WA	Multiple Bombings (2)	American Front Skinheads		
11/27-28/93	Chicago, IL	Firebombings (9)	Animal Liberation Front		
3-1-94	New York, NY	Shooting	Rashid Najib Baz	1	3
4-19-95	Oklahoma City, OK	Truck Bombing	Timothy McVeigh and Terry Nichols (Michael Fortier found guilty of failing to alert authorities of plot)	168	754
4-1-96	Spokane, WA	Pipe Bombing/Bank Robbery	Spokane Bank Robbers		
7-12-96	Spokane, WA	Pipe Bombing/Bank Robbery	Spokane Bank Robbers		
7-27-96	Atlanta, GA	Pipe Bombing	Eric Robert Rudolph	2	112
1-2-97	Washington, DC Leavenworth, KS	Letter Bombing (Counted as 1 incident)	Unknown		
1-16-97	Atlanta, GA	Bombing of Abortion Clinic	Eric Robert Rudolph		8

CHRONOLOGICAL SUMMARY OF
TERRORIST INCIDENTS IN THE UNITED STATES 1980-2005

DATE	LOCATION	INCIDENT TYPE	PERPETRATOR	KILLED	INJURED
2-21-97	Atlanta, GA	Bombing of Alternative Lifestyle Nightclub	Eric Robert Rudolph		5
1-29-98	Birmingham, AL	Bombing of Reproductive Services Clinic	Eric Robert Rudolph	1	1
3-31-98	Arecibo, PR	Bombing of Superaqueduct Construction Project	Ejercito Popular Boricua Macheteros		
6-9-98	Rio Piedras, PR	Bombing of Bank Branch Office	Ejercito Popular Boricua Macheteros		
6-25-98	Santa Isabel, PR	Bombing of Bank Branch Office	Ejercito Popular Boricua Macheteros suspected		1
6-27-98	Espanola, NM	Arson	Raymond Anthony Sandoval		
10-19-98	Vail, CO	Arson Fire at Ski Resort	Earth Liberation Front		
3-19-99	Santa Fe, NM	Attempted Bombing	Raymond Anthony Sandoval		
3-27-99	Franklin Township, NJ	Bombing of Circus Vehicles	Animal Liberation Front		
4-5-99	Minneapolis-St. Paul, MN	Malicious Destruction and Theft	Animal Liberation Front		
5-9-99	Eugene, OR	Bombing	Animal Liberation Front		
7/2-4/99	Chicago, IL Skokie, IL Northbrook, IL Bloomington, IN	Multiple Shootings	Benjamin Nathaniel Smith	2	8
8-10-99	Granada Hills, CA	Multiple Shootings	Buford O'Neal Furrow	1	5
8/28-29/99	Orange, CA	Malicious Destruction and Theft	Animal Liberation Front		
10-24-99	Bellingham, WA	Malicious Destruction and Theft	Animal Liberation Front		
11-20-99	Puyallup, WA	Malicious Destruction	Animal Liberation Front		
12-25-99	Monmouth, OR	Arson	Earth Liberation Front		
12-31-99	East Lansing, MI	Arson	Earth Liberation Front		
1-3-00	Petaluma, CA	Incendiary Attack	Animal Liberation Front		
1-15-00	Petaluma, CA	Incendiary Attack	Animal Liberation Front		
1-22-00	Bloomington, IN	Arson	Earth Liberation Front		
5-7-00	Olympia, WA	Arson	Revenge of the Trees		
7-2-00	North Vernon, IN	Arson	Animal Liberation Front		
7-20-00	Rhinelander, WI	Vandalism	Earth Liberation Front		

DATE	LOCATION	INCIDENT TYPE	PERPETRATOR	KILLED	INJURED
12-1-00	Phoenix, AZ	Multiple Arsons	Mark Warren Sands		
12/9-30/00	Suffolk County, Long Island, NY	Multiple Arsons	Earth Liberation Front		
1-2-01	Glendale, OR	Arson	Earth Liberation Front		
2-20-01	Visalia, CA	Arson	Earth Liberation Front		
3-9-01	Culpeper, VA	Tree Spiking	Earth Liberation Front		
3-30-01	Eugene, OR	Arson	Earth Liberation Front		
4-15-01	Portland, OR	Arson	Earth Liberation Front		
5-17-01	Harrisburg, PA	Bank Robbery	Clayton Lee Waagner		
5-21-01	Seattle, WA	Arson	Earth Liberation Front		
5-21-01	Clatskanie, OR	Arson	Earth Liberation Front		
7-24-01	Stateline, NV	Destruction of Property	Earth Liberation Front		
9-9-01	Morgantown, WV	Bank Robbery	Clayton Lee Waagner		
9-11-01	New York, NY Washington, DC New Cumberland, PA	Aircraft Attack	Al-Qa'ida	2972	est.12000
9/01-11/01	New York, NY Washington, DC Lantana, FL	*Bacillus anthracis* Mailings	Unknown	5	17
10-14-01	Litchfield, CA	Arson	Earth Liberation Front		
11-12-01	San Diego, CA	Burglary and Vandalism	Animal Liberation Front		
3-18-02	Erie, PA	Vandalism	Earth Liberation Front		
3-24-02	Erie, PA	Arson	Earth Liberation Front		
5/11-12/02	Harborcreek, PA	Vandalism/Destruction of Property	Earth Liberation Front/ Animal Liberation Front		
7-4-02	Los Angeles, CA	Shooting	Hesham Mohamed Ali Hedayat	2	
8/02-10/02	Henrico and Goochland Counties, VA	Vandalism and Destruction of Property	Earth Liberation Front		
8-11-02	Warren, PA	Arson	Earth Liberation Front		
9/15-16/02	Harborcreek, PA	Vandalism/Destruction of Property	Earth Liberation Front/ Animal Liberation Front		
11-26-02	Harborcreek, PA	Arson	Earth Liberation Front/ Animal Liberation Front		
1-1-03	Girard, PA	Arson	Earth Liberation Front		
3-3-03	Chico, CA	Vandalism	Animal Liberation Front		

CHRONOLOGICAL SUMMARY OF
TERRORIST INCIDENTS IN THE UNITED STATES 1980-2005

DATE	LOCATION	INCIDENT TYPE	PERPETRATOR	KILLED	INJURED
8/03-9/03	San Diego, CA	Arson	Earth Liberation Front		
8-22-03	West Covina, CA	Vandalism and Destruction of Property	Earth Liberation Front		
8-28-03	Emeryville, CA	Bombing	Daniel Andreas San Diego suspected		
9-26-03	Pleasanton, CA	Bombing	Daniel Andreas San Diego suspected		
1-19-04	Henrico County, VA	Arson	Earth Liberation Front suspected		
4-1-04	Oklahoma City, OK	Arson	Sean Michael Gillespie/Aryan Nations		
4-20-04	Redmond, WA	Vandalism and Arson	Earth Liberation Front		
5/04-7/04	Provo, UT	Vandalism and Arson	Animal Liberation Front		
12-27-04	Lincoln, CA	Attempted Arson	Earth Liberation Front		
1/05-2/05	Auburn, CA Sutter Creek, CA	Attempted Arson and Arson	Earth Liberation Front		
4-13-05	Sammanish, WA	Arson	Earth Liberation Front		
7-7-05	Los Angeles, CA	Attempted Arson	Animal rights extremists suspected		
9-16-05	Los Angeles, CA	Attempted Arson	Animal Liberation Front		
11-20-05	Hagerstown, MD	Arson	Earth Liberation Front		

TERRORISM
2002–2005